Thirty Years of the
Poetry Book Society 1956–1986

Thirty Years of the Poetry Book Society 1956–1986

Edited by Jonathan Barker

Preface by Blake Morrison

Hutchinson

London   Melbourne   Auckland   Johannesburg

This edition first published in 1988 by Hutchinson Ltd, an imprint of
Century Hutchinson Ltd, Brookmount House, 62–65 Chandos Place,
London WC2N 4NW, and by the Poetry Book Society Ltd, 21 Earls Court
Square, London SW5 9DE

Century Hutchinson Australia (Pty) Ltd,
PO Box 496, 16–22 Church Street, Hawthorn, Melbourne, Victoria 3122

Century Hutchinson New Zealand Ltd,
PO Box 40–086, 32–34 View Road, Glenfield, Auckland, 10

Century Hutchinson South Africa (Pty) Ltd,
PO Box 337, Bergvlei 2012, South Africa

Set in Linotron Bembo by
Rowland Phototypesetting Ltd,
Bury St Edmunds, Suffolk

Printed and bound in Great Britain by
Butler & Tanner Ltd, Frome and London

British Library Cataloguing in Publication Data
Thirty Years of the Poetry Book Society.
  1. English poetry—20th century
  I. Barker, Jonathan, *1949–*   II. Poetry
Book Society
821′.914′08   PR1225

ISBN 0-09-171041-3

Contents

6

Preface

Here is an anthology which defines itself more by what it's not than what it is. It isn't a collection with a theme or subject; it isn't a selection from a journal or little magazine; it isn't trying to represent a genre or a gender, a culture or a sub-culture; it isn't a manifesto intended to change the world. A random selection of poems loosely associated with the Poetry Book Society, itself a loose association – it claims to be no more than that. This randomness, I'm tempted to say, is precisely its strength, and all the stronger for not being so random as it intends. The first poem is by Kingsley Amis, published in the year of *New Lines*; the last is by Craig Raine, published thirty years later; both are domestic poems, taking in their washing and looking no further than their back gardens, though one poem ends with an angry snarl and the other with a lyric sigh. So, 'From the Movement to the Martians' might make a subtitle for this anthology, if it weren't that so much of what comes in-between, diverse and stubbornly individual as it is, doesn't serve (and wouldn't want to) as the filling for such a neat literary- historical sandwich.

T. S. Eliot was one of the first directors of the Poetry Book Society. He is represented here not by a poem but by two fugitive prose items – appropriately so, since by 1956 his critical-administrative influence was more in evidence than his poetic. The Georgianism he was supposed to have banished can be seen in the contributions of de la Mare (who died that year at the age of 83), Graves, Day Lewis, Betjeman and William Plomer. It had never really gone away: Auden (who's here too) had restored connections with the pre-1914 tradition. Georgianism in its best sense – downbeat, socially realistic, local, anecdotal, metrically accomplished – can be found throughout this anthology; the dissenting wild men (George Barker and Michael Hastings prominent among them) can be counted on one hand. Is this the conservatism of the PBS or of the times? Hard to say – the pleasures of this anthology are not in any case to be found in seeking literary-historical patterns, but in turning up poems not come across before or long forgotten or (like Lowell's 'For the Union Dead', Larkin's 'Waiting for Breakfast' and Hughes's 'You Hated Spain') never so familiar as to withhold some new surprise.

Even more pleasurable are the prose pieces: poets rarely issue statements about their work, least of all when their books are first published, so these specially commissioned apologias are unique, another small PBS service to posterity. Not that the poets are always forthcoming: 'once I have said that the poems were written in or near Hull, Yorkshire, with a succession of Royal Sovereign 2B pencils during the years 1955 to 1963, there seems little to add,' says Larkin about *The Whitsun Weddings*. But he then, of course, goes on to add a great deal, especially about poetic composition, ending on a Dockery-like, grandly fatalistic note: 'The only consolation in the whole business, as in just about every other, is that in all probability there was really no choice.' His contribution is in dialogue with Betjeman's on *Summoned by Bells* four years earlier. 'I have never thought one subject more "poetical" than another', says Betjeman; Larkin agrees with this, using the same cautionary quote marks ('Nowadays nobody believes in "poetic" subjects'), but then disagrees: 'The longer one goes on . . . the more one feels that some subjects *are* more poetic than others, if only that poems about them get written whereas poems about other subjects don't.' Douglas Dunn on *Terry Street* ('It was never my intention that the poems be read as social or any other kind of protest'), Thom Gunn on *Moly* ('it could be seen as a history of San Francisco from 1965–1969'), Seamus Heaney on *North* ('The second section is the result of a need to be explicit about pressures and prejudices watermarked into the psyche of anyone born and bred in Northern Ireland'), – each throws fascinating light on the author or the work.

In making a selection from thirty years of poetry and prose, Jonathan Barker has clearly been spoilt for choice. But he hasn't spoilt things for the reader, by being either too exclusive or too undiscriminating. It's an unusual, at times exasperating but finally seductive anthology.

Blake Morrison

Introduction

Since 1954 the Poetry Book Society, with Arts Council subsidy, has distributed four quarterly Choices to members each year. The Choice is always a book of new poems, and with it members receive a quarterly *Bulletin* containing an exclusive prose contribution from the author of the book, and also prose on, and poems from, any other books recommended that quarter. The Choice and Recommendations are decided before publication by selectors appointed by the Board of Management. Each year since 1956 the PBS has also published an annual winter anthology of new poems (until recently known as the 'Supplement') compiled of late by an editor who is a retiring selector. In 1986 the PBS had the idea of making the annual anthology available to the general public as well as to its members, and arranged for Century Hutchinson to publish it for them. The book sold out in three months and was swiftly reprinted.

For this selection from thirty years of the *Bulletin* and annual anthology, I have also included a selection of poems commissioned for the poetry festivals organized by the PBS in the early sixties, and which eventually evolved into the hugely successful annual Poetry Internationals directed variously by Ted Hughes, Patrick Garland and Charles Osborne. My selection from the original prose has inevitably been influenced by Eric W. White's 1979 anthology made for members from twenty-five years of prose contributions to the *Bulletin*, but rather than select exclusively from Eric's impressive choice I have included some alternatives as well. I have also, of course, been able to add prose from *Bulletins* published since then. I have tried to include prose comments by poets which stand on their own and, I hope, will make sense to readers who might not have the books concerned to hand.

When it comes to the selection of poems, I have in the main kept my choice to those first published by the PBS, but where a poet has subsequently revised a poem I have printed the later version. The poems selected for the annual anthologies by numerous distinguished editors were invariably first published there. My respect for the editorial intelligence of these editors is large: each one managed somehow to represent a survey of the best of poetry in his or her day, and I hope my selection from their work is reasonably sensitive. None the less I have had to be rigorously selective in order to condense thirty years of material into one book. I have included fewer poems from the quarterly *Bulletins* for the simple reason that, with some exceptions, poems were included there specifically to attract attention to the simultaneously published quarterly Recommendation in which they appeared. However, I do include poems occasionally first published in the *Bulletins* and a number of others I thought too good to miss.

This is, by definition, a personal selection, but one which is as objective as I can make it. As requested, I have endeavoured to provide a balance of work from the thirty years to represent changing developments and a range of styles, but some years provided me with such a rich hoard I was unable to resist giving them precedence. My main criteria in selecting the work were that the poems and prose must be good, they must be enjoyable, and they must also work in their new context of this anthology. I should stress again the large amount of work of high quality from which I have made the selection. This has led inevitably to exclusions, especially amongst the prose, the longer poems, and work by a number of younger poets whom I should have liked to represent. Some poets contributed fine poems to many anthologies, so selecting just one was difficult. Moreover the need for balance over the years means some poets have had to be represented here by their earlier, rather than more recent, work. I am grateful to those publishers and sometimes poets listed in the acknowledgments who gave permission for work to appear here. In a number of cases, alas, permission could not be obtained for work I would have liked to include. I am also grateful to Blake Morrison, former Chairman of the PBS, who read through the typescript and suggested deletions and a few additions.

Jonathan Barker

1956

Kingsley Amis

Creeper

Shaving this morning, I look out of the window
In expectation: will another small
Tendril of ivy, dry and straw-yellow,
Have put its thin clasp on the garden wall?

Oh dear no. A few arid strands, a few
Curled-up leaves, are all that's left of it.
The children pulled it up for something to do.
My mouth sets in its usual post-box slit.

Fled is that vision of a bottle-green
Fur-coat of foliage muffling the pale brick,
Stamping into the flat suburban scene
A proof of beauty, lovable exotic.

Of course, I know ivy will sweetly plump
Itself all over, shyly barge into crannies,
Pull down lump after elegiac lump,
Then tastefully screen ruin from our eyes.

Then it would all become a legal quibble:
Whose what has wrecked what how and by whose what;
And moral: is turning stout wall to rubble
A fool's trick in fact, but not in thought?

We should be thankful to be spared all that
When bank-clerk longings get a short answer,
When someone snatches off our silly hat
And drop-kicks it under a steamroller.

13

C. Day Lewis

Lot 96

Lot 96: a brass-rimmed ironwork fender.
It had stood guard for years, where it used to belong,
Over the hearth of a couple who loved tenderly.
Now it will go for a song.

Night upon winter night, as she gossiped with him
Or was silent, he watched the talkative firelight send
Its reflections twittering over that burnished rim
Like a language of world without end.

Death, which unclasped their hearts, dismantled all.
The world they made is as if it had never been true –
That firelit bubble of warmth, serene, magical,
Ageless in form and hue.

Now there stands, dulled in an auction room,
This iron thing – a far too durable irony,
Reflecting never a ghost of the lives that illumed it,
No hint of the sacred fire.

This lot was part of their precious bond, almost
A property of its meaning. Here, in the litter
Washed up by death, values are reassessed
At a nod from the highest bidder.

Walter de la Mare

Shepherd's Warning

Pleasant it was, once – once to stray
Through the antique woods,
The primeval May,
Heedless of morrow or yesterday.

Nor even to think,
As we went our way,
The World was skirting a Future's brink
That might shatter and wrench it link from link.

What cause to question? – to pause in surmise?
Save that sullen red in the eastern skies?

Walter de la Mare

Ulysses

There was a high ship sailed the main,
Masts to the stars sailed she:
Not a wraith of foam 'neath her figurehead shone
So still was the sea.

Happier the landsman with care distraught
Than mariners winds may cheat,
While the mouths of the guileful sea-maids chant
Lament, and the sea-bells beat

A solemn resounding knell, and call
Their souls from their bodies, and wake
A thirst in the eyes no beauty on earth
Hath power to slake.

T. S. Eliot

Poetry and the Schools

I have never been very much in favour of introducing the work of living authors into school curricula of the study of English literature, for two reasons. First, I think that schoolboys and girls should be given a background of the classic authors of our language whose work is part of history and can be taught as such. Second, I think that all growing boys and girls should have an area of literature which they're not taught anything about, on which they don't have to pass any examinations, in which they can make their own discoveries, their own errors, and learn for themselves. If every secondary school in the country joined the Poetry Book Society and had a shelf in its library exhibiting the books of new poetry, this year and last year and several years, and just left them there for the boys and girls in the upper forms to discover for themselves and find out what they liked, we would be doing a very great service, because it is in the years between fourteen and eighteen if ever that people become readers of poetry and lovers of poetry, and also amongst those readers will be the poets of that generation. I think every poet has been a reader of poetry before he has been inflamed with the desire to become a writer of poetry, and it is a good thing also that boys and girls of that age should learn to think of poetry as a living art, as something which is still being written and which will be written in their own generation. I have always held firmly that a nation which ceases to produce poetry will in the long run cease to be able to enjoy and even understand the great poetry of its own past.

Philip Larkin

Waiting for Breakfast

Waiting for breakfast, while she brushed her hair,
I looked down at the empty hotel yard
Once meant for coaches. Cobblestones were wet,
But sent no light back to the loaded sky,
Sunk as it was with mist down to the roofs.
Drainpipes and fire-escape climbed up
Past rooms still burning their electric light:
I thought: Featureless morning, featureless night.

Misjudgment: for the stones slept, and the mist
Wandered absolvingly past all it touched,
Yet hung like a stayed breath; the lights burnt on,
Pinpoints of undisturbed excitement; beyond the glass
The colourless vial of day painlessly spilled
My world back after a year, my lost lost world
Like a cropping deer strayed near my path again,
Bewaring the mind's least clutch. Turning, I kissed her,
Easily for sheer joy tipping the balance to love.

But, tender visiting,
Fallow as a deer or an unforced field,
How would you have me? Towards your grace
My promises meet and lock and race like rivers,
But only when you choose. Are you jealous of her?
Will you refuse to come till I have sent
Her terribly away, importantly live
Part invalid, part baby, and part saint?

Vernon Watkins

Demands of the Poet

I set my heart against all lesser toil.
Speak to me now more closely than the birds.
That labour done, on which I spent my oil,
Avails me nothing till you test the words.

How much the beating pulse may hold the years
Yet write the athletic wisdom on the page
You alone say. You bring the authentic tears
Which recognize the moment without age.

No lesser vision gives me consolation.
Wealth is a barren waste, that spring forgot.
Art is the principle of all creation,
And there the desert is, where art is not.

1957

W. H. Auden

The More Loving One

Looking up at the stars, I know quite well
That, for all they care, I can go to hell,
But on earth indifference is the least
We have to dread from man or beast.

How should we like it were stars to burn
With a passion for us we could not return?
If equal affection cannot be,
Let the more loving one be me.

Admirer as I think I am
Of stars that do not give a damn,
I cannot, now I see them, say
I missed one terribly all day.

Were all stars to disappear or die,
I should learn to look at an empty sky
And feel its total dark sublime,
Though this might take me a little time.

Norman Cameron

The Compassionate Fool

My enemy had bidden me as guest.
His table all set out with wine and cake,
His ordered chairs, he to beguile me dressed
So neatly, moved my pity for his sake.

I knew it was an ambush, but could not
Leave him to eat his cake up by himself
And put his unused glasses on the shelf.
I made pretence of falling in his plot,

And trembled when in his anxiety
He bared it too absurdly to my view.
And even as he stabbed me through and through
I pitied him for his small strategy.

Ted Hughes

Everyman's Odyssey

Telemachus, now to remember your coming of age.
Years your trust was open as the doors of your house
To the boisterous princes, all so phrasing your mother,
So cushioning the going of her feet with the glow of their eyes,
Who brought such trinkets, and hoisted the jugglers and the
                                                      dancers
Onto the protesting trestles of your tables.

Your mother, white, a woe freezing a silence,
Parried long their impertinence with her shuttle,
And such after-banquet belching of adulation
Through your hoop and handball years. O Telemachus
Remember the day you saw the spears on the wall
And their great blades shook light at you like the sea.

If these memories move at all in your ghost
This last must open up a wound: recall that year
You sulked among the suitors – too big for their comfort
And yet too few for their fear. Your father's honour
Was a sword in the scabbard of your body you could not draw,
What patience you had a slow bird quartering the seas.

But avenge yourself on recalling that. I would hear
How the father arrives out of the bottom of the world.
I would see one of the beggars that brawl on my porch
Reach hands to the bow hardly to be strung by man –
I would see these gluttons, guests by grace of their numbers,
Flung through the doors with their bellies full of arrows.

Louis MacNeice on

Visitations

(Faber & Faber) 1957

I feel delighted and honoured that the Poetry Book Society have chosen my book, *Visitations*. This is the first book of short poems I have published since 1948. In between I have published *Ten Burnt Offerings* (ten long poems which were experiments in dialectical structure) and one very long poem, *Autumn Sequel*, the point of which was missed by most of the book-reviewers; it was 'occasional' but not casual, being an attempt to marry myth to 'actuality'. While writing these longer pieces I was incapable of writing short ones. When the lyrical impulse did return, this interval of abstention, it seems to me, had caused certain changes in my lyric-writing – I naturally hope for the better. It is hard to put labels on one's own work but I like to think that my latest short poems are on the whole more concentrated and better organized than my earlier ones, relying more on syntax and bony feature than on bloom or frill or the floating image. I should also like to think that sometimes they achieve a blend of 'classical' and 'romantic', marrying the element of wit to the sensuous-mystical element.

So much for my own poems. Now, as to 'poetry in general' – there is, strictly speaking, no such thing, every poem being a concrete individual. Still, one *can* generalize about these individuals. I hold that poetry, far from being a release of gas, is more like a precision instrument – one that can be used where that other precision instrument, science, is completely and for ever useless. That is, I agree with the late Christopher Caudwell that poetry is inevitably subjective – but this need not imply either imprecision or isolation; as Caudwell pointed out, the poet retires into his inner world thereby to re-establish communion with his fellows (not all his fellows, or course, but a worthwhile number). So long as hunger remains as real as bread, this will be an important activity. As for my own preferences, I like a poem to exist on more than one plane; I hope this is true even of my own 'poems of place' (there are several such in *Visitations*) which, superficially, are merely descriptive pieces. I also think a poet should not be afraid of being thought either sentimental or vulgar. Lastly, we should always remember that, while a good poem cannot but be an artefact, it is also certainly an organism.

1958

Stevie Smith

Heartless

My little dog is called
Heartless,
His nature is
Heartless,
Yet when he barks he cries
'Heartless, heartless',
And this is a complaint,

So perhaps he will improve,
. . . one day learn to love?

'Heartless!', I call,
But he barks again
'Heartless, heartless'
Only to complain.

I hope he finds where it is love is lacking,
And stops barking.

Temple

a temple drifts
Through three clouds of moss -
Aslant across a path
            the tree scatters
A single leaf
            (precisely,
as I dot this i)

*

Stele (Athens Museum)

See my daughter's dear child whom I
            hold in my lap - thus
I held him before in   those days
When with living eyes we looked out on
            the sun — now
He's dead, I hold him here still - because I
am dead also.

*

HIROSHIMA REBUILT

A town can be rebuilt but not the wreck
Of the sky in the mind - bombed by a cloud
- -   - -   -   -   -

        Stephen. Spender

A. S. J. Tessimond (after the French of Jacques Prévert)

Food for Thought
(La Grasse Matinée)

It's a terrible thing
the small noise of a hard-boiled egg being cracked on a metal
                                                        counter
when it rings in the memory
the mind of a hungry man
and it's a terrible thing the face of the man
the face of the man who is hungry
when he looks at himself at six in the morning
in the glass of the big shop window
and sees a face the colour of dust
yet it isn't his head that he looks at
in the grocer's window
he doesn't care a damn for that human head of his
doesn't give it a thought
he dreams
he has a vision of another head
a calf's head perhaps
with vinegar sauce
or any sort of head that can be eaten
and gently he moves his jaws
very gently
and gently he grinds his teeth
for the world is laughing at him laughing its head off
he counts on his fingers one two three
one two three
it's three days since he has eaten
and it's no good telling and telling himself for three days
It can't go on
for it does go on
three days
three nights
without eating
and behind these shop windows
are these pies these bottles these jars

27

these dead fish protected by tins
these tins protected by windows
these windows protected by policemen
these policemen protected by men's fear
what fortifications for six unfortunate sardines! . . .
A little further on is the café
coffee-and-cream and fresh rolls
the man lurches along
and inside his head
a cloud of words
a cloud of words
sardines on toast
hard-boiled egg coffee and cream
coffee with a dash of rum
coffee and cream
coffee and cream
coffee and crime with a dash of blood! . . .
a man well-thought-of in his neighbourhood
has had his throat cut in broad daylight
the murderer robbed him of
one and ten
that's one coffee with a dash of rum
at a shilling
and two buttered rolls
and twopence for the waiter's tip

It's a terrible thing
the small noise of a hard-boiled egg
being cracked on a metal counter
it's a terrible noise
when it rings in the memory
the mind of a hungry man

1959

Edwin Muir

The Strange Return

Behind him Hell sank in the plain.
He saw far off the liquid glaze
Of burning somewhere. That was all.
A burning there or in his brain?
He could not tell. His was a case,
He thought, that put all Hell in doubt,
Though he had cause to know that place.
Had They some darker thought in mind,
Arranged his flight, inveigled him out
To walk halfway from Heaven to Hell?
Was where he stood a dream of stone?
No matter, he was here alone.
And then he saw the tangled skein,
His footprints following him behind
And stretching to the prison lock,
And there two towers like ears a-cock.
Would they answer to his knock,
Brush all aside, invite him in,
Crack a dry witticism on sin,
Excuse his saunter over the sand,
If he returned? Or understand?
But then the towers like ears a-cock.

How from that bastion could he fall
Like Lazarus backwards into life
And travel to another death?
And now in buried distances
There was a wakening and he heard
Word at odds with common word,
A child's voice crying, 'Let me be!'
In a world he could not touch,
And others saying, 'Be in time',
With such a strange anxiety
(And he himself caught here in time).
The young girl's brow, the vertical cleft
Above the eyes that saw too much
Too soon: how could he counter these,
Make friends with the evils, take his part,
Salute the outer and inner strife,
The bickering between doubt and faith,
Inherit the tangle he had left,
Outface the trembling at his heart?

Three feet away a little tree
Put out in pain a single bud
That did not fear the ultimate fire.
And in a flash he knew it all,
The long-forgotten and new desire,
And looked and saw the tree was good.

Alastair Reid

Outlook, Uncertain

No season
brings conclusion.

Each year,
through heartache, nightmare,

true loves alter,
marriages falter,

and lovers illumine
the antique design,

apart, together,
foolish as weather,

right as rain,
sure as ruin.

Must you, then, and I
adjust the whole sky

over every morning?
Or else, submitting

to cloud and storm,
enact the same

lugubrious ending,
new lives pending?

1960

John Betjeman on

Summoned by Bells

(John Murray) 1960

I have written verse for as long as I can remember. I have always preferred reading poetry to reading prose which is why I have found reviewing such an odious task – I read out loud to myself and cannot skip and this causes me to read slowly.

If we are influenced by the first poetry we read after the nursery rhymes we all know, I was influenced by W. E. Henley's *Lyra Heroica* which I was given at the age of about six or seven. I would not read blank verse in those days as I considered not using rhyme was cheating. I used to think then that you merely had to have the same number of syllables in each successive line to make correct scansion. I didn't find out about stress till I was about thirteen.

I have never thought one subject more 'poetical' than another, but have delighted in the niceties of rhyme and rhythm and choosing certain metres and rhyming schemes to suit certain subjects. A place or a moment recalls a mood I want to put down. A line comes to me. It gives me the beginnings of the rhythm for the poem. I put down the line on the nearest available bit of paper – the back of a cigarette packet or a letter (which consequently doesn't get answered) and think about the rest of the poem in trains, driving a motor car, bicycling or walking – wherever I can be alone and recite the words out loud until they seem to be the right ones in the right order. I write very slowly and copy the completed draft out five or six times before I am contented with it. Once this process is over, I am no longer interested in the verse.

I think everyone is a poet when young and that hearing and reading so much prose drives the poetry in most people underground. It then wells up again in the vast public memory for the words of popular songs. Much of my own verse has been written to the tunes of the English

Hymnal and *Hymns A. & M.* which are part of my heritage.

The fact that my verse has sold so well strikes me as lucky and miraculous for I think many living poets are better than I am. Please accept my thanks for choosing this blank verse autobiography.

Robert Lowell

For the Union Dead

"Relinquunt Omnia Servare Rem Publicam."

The old South Boston Aquarium stands
in a Sahara of snow now. Its broken windows are boarded.
The bronze weathervane cod has lost half its scales.
The airy tanks are dry.

Once my nose crawled like a snail on the glass;
my hand tingled
to burst the bubbles
drifting from the noses of the cowed, compliant fish.

My hand draws back. I often sigh still
for the dark downward and vegetating kingdom
of the fish and reptile. One morning last March,
I pressed against the new barbed and galvanized

fence on the Boston Common. Behind their cage,
yellow dinosaur steamshovels were grunting
as they cropped up tons of mush and grass
to gouge their underworld garage.

Parking spaces luxuriate like civic
sandpiles in the heart of Boston.
A girdle of orange, Puritan-pumpkin colored girders
braces the tingling Statehouse,

shaking over the excavations, as it faces Colonel Shaw
and his bell-cheeked Negro infantry
on St. Gaudens' shaking Civil War relief,
propped by a plank splint against the garage's earthquake.

Two months after marching through Boston,
half the regiment was dead;
at the dedication,
William James could almost hear the bronze Negroes breathe.

Their monument sticks like a fishbone
in the city's throat.
Its Colonel is as lean
as a compass-needle.

He has an angry wrenlike vigilance,
a greyhound's gentle tautness;
he seems to wince at pleasure,
and suffocate for privacy.

He is out of bounds now. He rejoices in man's lovely,
peculiar power to choose life and die –
when he leads his black soldiers to death,
he cannot bend his back.

On a thousand small town New England greens,
the old white churches hold their air
of sparse, sincere rebellion; frayed flags
quilt the graveyards of the Grand Army of the Republic.

The stone statues of the abstract Union Soldier
grow slimmer and younger each year –
wasp-waisted, they doze over muskets
and muse through their sideburns. . .

Shaw's father wanted no monument
except the ditch,
where his son's body was thrown
and lost with his 'niggers.'

The ditch is nearer.
There are no statues for the last war here;
on Boyleston Street, a commercial photograph
shows Hiroshima boiling

over a Mosler Safe, the 'Rock of Ages'
that survived the blast. Space is nearer.
When I crouch to my television set,
the drained faces of Negro school-children rise like balloons.

Colonel Shaw
is riding on his bubble,
he waits
for the blesséd break.

The Aquarium is gone. Everywhere,
giant finned cars nose forward like fish;
a savage servility
slides by on grease.

1961

Louis MacNeice

The Truisms

His father gave him a box of truisms
Shaped like a coffin, then his father died;
The truisms remained on the mantelpiece
As wooden as the playbox they had been packed in
Or that other his father skulked inside.

Then he left home, left the truisms behind him
Still on the mantelpiece, met love, met war,
Sordor, disappointment, defeat, betrayal,
Till through disbeliefs he arrived at a house
He could not remember seeing before,

And he walked straight in; it was where he had come from
And something told him the way to behave.
He raised his hand and blessed his home;
The truisms flew and perched on his shoulders
And a tall tree sprouted from his father's grave.

Sylvia Plath

Tulips

The tulips are too excitable, it is winter here.
Look how white everything is, how quiet, how snowed-in.
I am learning peacefulness, lying by myself quietly
As the light lies on these white walls, this bed, these hands.
I am nobody; I have nothing to do with explosions.
I have given my name and my day-clothes up to the nurses
And my history to the anesthetist and my body to surgeons.

They have propped my head between the pillow and the sheet-
          cuff
Like an eye between two white lids that will not shut.
Stupid pupil, it has to take everything in.
The nurses pass and pass, they are no trouble,
They pass the way gulls pass inland in their white caps,
Doing things with their hands, one just the same as another,
So it is impossible to tell how many there are.

My body is a pebble to them, they tend it as water
Tends to the pebbles it must run over, smoothing them gently.
They bring me numbness in their bright needles, they bring me
          sleep.
Now I have lost myself I am sick of baggage –
My patent leather overnight case like a black pillbox,
My husband and child smiling out of the family photo;
Their smiles catch onto my skin, little smiling hooks.

I have let things slip, a thirty-year-old cargo boat
Stubbornly hanging on to my name and address.
They have swabbed me clear of my loving associations.
Scared and bare on the green plastic-pillowed trolley
I watched my teaset, my bureaus of linen, my books
Sink out of sight, and the water went over my head.
I am a nun now, I have never been so pure.

I didn't want any flowers, I only wanted
To lie with my hands turned up and be utterly empty.
How free it is, you have no idea how free –
The peacefulness is so big it dazes you,
And it asks nothing, a name tag, a few trinkets.
It is what the dead close on, finally; I imagine them
Shutting their mouths on it, like a Communion tablet.

The tulips are too red in the first place, they hurt me.
Even through the gift paper I could hear them breathe
Lightly, through their white swaddlings, like an awful baby.
Their redness talks to my wound, it corresponds.
They are subtle: they seem to float, though they weigh me down,
Upsetting me with their sudden tongues and their color,
A dozen red lead sinkers round my neck.

Nobody watched me before, now I am watched.
The tulips turn to me, and the window behind me
Where once a day the light slowly widens and slowly thins,
And I see myself, flat, ridiculous, a cut-paper shadow
Between the eye of the sun and the eyes of the tulips,
And I have no face, I have wanted to efface myself.
The vivid tulips eat my oxygen.

Before they came the air was calm enough,
Coming and going, breath by breath, without any fuss.
Then the tulips filled it up like a loud noise.
Now the air snags and eddies round them the way a river
Snags and eddies round a sunken rust-red engine.
They concentrate my attention, that was happy
Playing and resting without committing itself.

The walls, also, seem to be warming themselves.
The tulips should be behind bars like dangerous animals;
They are opening like the mouth of some great African cat,
And I am aware of my heart: it opens and closes
Its bowl of red blooms out of sheer love of me.
The water I taste is warm and salt, like the sea,
And comes from a country far away as health.

1962

George Barker on

The View from a Blind I

(Faber & Faber) 1962

Nearly all the poems in this book got themselves written in ten weeks during the spring of 1961. I could hope that they are a bit simpler in style and a bit better in character and a bit less blowsy than their predecessors. Rome seems to me an extraordinarily good place for poems, just as some spots are good for mushrooms. When I came here I knew that I had simply to get up in the morning and collect the verses. I was continually reminded of John Clare's remark when they asked him where he got his poems. He said: 'I went out into the fields and found them there.' And so, for what they are, I found the poems in this book skulking among the fallen masonry of Trajan's Forum, or growing out of the Altar of Cæsar, or lifting their hind legs against the pillars of Apollo. Now I wonder if it might not be simply a question of finding out where poems are, for surely it would be misguided to look for the Lyre Bird in a museum (that specimen in the Natural History Museum in South Kensington is dead) or for the Muse herself in the London Library? But however that may be (what the hell, Mehitabel) I was grateful for being given these poems (that is, the good ones; the dud ones I stole; but that's that) because, like all other poets, as I believe, who have sat around for far too long with their faculties furled, I had thought never again to be revisited by the donative powers, if, indeed, I have ever been visited by them. I may not have honoured their gifts; but I think I was visited. And if these terms of speech seem pretentious, and I suppose that they are, for one is hinting of a matter about which no one knows anything, I cannot think that these terms are much more pretentious than any others in which one might speak. Even Valéry's image of the white-coated poet as scientist appears now to be a claim of transcendental and even apocalyptic proportions. What can one say? A man does not invent poems; they discover him.

Robert Graves on

New Poems 1962
(Cassell) 1962

I have been publishing poems since the year 1909, since when I have watched a great many changes in fashion – names suddenly made and suddenly lost again, with here and there a real poet writing whom nobody pays much attention to, but who doesn't care because he's not competing with anyone but himself. It will always be that way.

The history of English poetry is traced in textbooks as a succession of movements or schools – the School of Chaucer, the Allegorical School, the early Tudor Dramatists, the Euphuists and so on, past the anti-Jacobins, the Lake School, the mid-Victorian romantics, until one reaches the Georgians, the Imagists and the Modernist Movement, for which the bell is now tolling. But schools and movements are fictions. If a school, meaning the disciples and imitators of a particular verse-craftsman or technician, achieves newspaper renown, this is a grave criticism of his sincerity. A poet should be inimitable. When two real poets recognize each other as true to their common vocation, this will only accentuate the difference between them in rhythm, diction and the rest. Any talk of a 'school' means that someone is peddling a new technique of verbal conjuring; as in commercial schools that teach writers of advertising copy how to make easily hypnotizable subjects believe what they themselves never believe in. Craftsmanship is self taught by the poet's service to the Muse: who is unpossessable and never satisfied.

A poet needs constant discouragement. I like to think that this Poetry Book Society choice of my new poems is a simple act of almsgiving: and indeed, not having been gainfully employed or licked an insurance stamp in all my life, I am unentitled to the Old Age Pension.

41

Robert Graves

The Meeting

We, two elementals, woman and man,
Approached each other from far away:
I on the lower wind, she on the upper.

And the faith with which we came invested
By the blind thousands of our twin worlds
Formed thunder clouds about us.

Never such uproar as when we met,
Nor such forked lightning; rain in a cataract
Tumbled on deserts dry these thousand years.

What of the meteorologists?
They said nothing, turned their faces away,
Let the event pass unrecorded.

And what of us? We also said nothing.
Is it not the height of silent humour
To cause an unknown change in the earth's climate?

Ian Hamilton

Windfalls

The windfalls ripen on the lawn,
The flies won't be disturbed.
They doze and glisten,
They wait for the fresh falls
To wipe them out. Like warts,
A pair of them sleep on your wrist.
Disabled, sleek, they have their fill.

Another wind prepares. It will shake apples
For these suicidal flies. It will restore
To lethargy your pale, disfigured hand.

Edwin Morgan

The Old Man and the Sea

And a white mist rolled out of the Pacific
and crept over the sand, stirring nothing –
cold, cold as nothing is cold
on those living highways, moved in
over the early morning trucks,
chilling the drivers in their cabins
(one stops for a paper cup
of coffee, stares out through the steam
at the mist, his hands on the warm cup
imagine the coldness, he throws out the cup
and swears as the fog rolls in, drives on
frowning to feel its touch on his face) –
and seagulls came to shriek at cockcrow
swooping through the wakening farms,
and the smoke struggled from the lumber camps
up into the smoke from the sea,
hovered in the sunless morning
as a lumberman whistled at the pump,
and sea-mist took the flash from the axe.
And above the still lakes of Oregon
and the Blue Mountains into Idaho
eastward, white wings brushing the forests,
a white finger probing the canyon
by Wood River, delicate, persistent, at last
finding by the half-light, in a house of stone,
a white-bearded man like an old sea-captain
cleaning a gun. – Keep back the sea,
keep back the sea! No reassurance
in that daybreak with no sun,
his blood thin, flesh patched and scarred,
eyes grown weary of hunting
and the great game all uncaught.
It was too late to fight the sea.
The raised barrel hardly gleamed
in that American valley, the shot

insulted the morning, crude and quick
with the end of a great writer's life –
fumbling nothing, but leaving questions
that echo beyond Spain and Africa.
Questions, not answers, chill the heart here,
a chained dog whining in the straw,
the gunsmoke marrying the sea-mist,
and silence of the inhuman valleys.

T. S. Eliot introduces the programme of the PBS Festival of Poetry, 1963

For the last thirty-eight years I have been concerned with the publication of poetry, and during that time I have, I believe, acquired as much knowledge of the public for poetry, and of the market for the work of new poets, as anyone still active in the world of letters. Interest in poetry, and in the work of younger poets, is certainly more widespread than it was in the twenties. Poetry prizes get more attention, and, owing to the wireless as well as to public poetry readings, many more people must have become accustomed to the sound of verse. But it remains true that the number of people capable of appreciating the new and unusual – capable of distinguishing between the significant and the negligible – and, what is more, with confidence in their own taste – remains very small. The reputation of a poet spreads very slowly: a younger generation may never realize that some poet now famous in their eyes may have waited for years before his work was known to more than a very small audience, and that it may have had to be fought for by a very few enthusiasts.

In the early stages a poet may have had the advantage of two supports: the 'little magazine' and the 'little publisher'. By the latter, I mean the small press which confines itself to the publication of new poets still unknown – the press which, owing perhaps to the devotion of one generous person, is on the lookout for new talent and is prepared to back it at a loss. Little magazines and little publishers come and go, but it would be a sad day when they vanished altogether. For the larger public capable of enjoying the work of young poets needs some assurance, not necessarily of notable success, but at least of the approval of critics in high places.

It was with such reflections in mind that I welcomed the foundation of the Poetry Book Society and became one of its original directors. It is with such reflections in mind that, having taken no part in the conduct of the Society for some years, I am happy to associate myself with its Festival by attesting my enduring interest in the cause for which it was founded.

Gavin Ewart

Huckstep

Huckstep was the groundsman at my prep school.
He put the heavy roller over the pitch,
Dragged by a horse in large flat leather shoes,
In those long-vanished summers.
A handsome smiling man and sunburned; quiet;
The brownest man I'd ever seen,
Dark oily hair and powerful arms in shirt sleeves.
He played, somebody told me, for the Kent Second
                                                    Eleven,
Certainly he bowled at us in the nets,
Left arm medium, round the wicket,
With a beautiful action, a back-tossed lock of hair.

Now that I've been 'literary' for so many years
I recognize him. He might have been
Lady Chatterley's lover, Ted in *The Go-Between*,
The natural man. A Kentish yeoman
Who even then charmed me with his grace –
So that for ever I shall see him bowling,
Picture the wheeling arm, the fluent action.
His name is one of those like 'Adlestrop'
That, once absorbed, can never be forgotten.
Huckstep. We all admired him.
And who, if he was as I think he was, would not?
There is a place in life for simple people.

Michael Hastings

The Middle Classes Have no Hero

The middle classes have no hero, who
Must be their hero? I must. When I rode
Down express missive by train from Derby,
To an aunt who to stay with for ever
In Herne Bay at war – the barrels of sound
Thrust stutters of steel into the night jive –
I sat down a dull moment practising
With a toddler's fervor shallow dreams where
Soft sand and swept breakwaters filled my toes.
Uncle – I was told was slaying dragons.

I watched through the blind in blackout winks from
The pier spread slumped beneath laid sandbags,
Like a child's sled sunk into the darkness.
At night the planes' ack-ack and buzzsaw ceased;
The cajole of a comedian begged
The troops sit up and howl to the last dog.
Amongst this barrage of accord somewhere
Sang my Father in his three stripes and blue
About to die weeks away on Cologne.
He too, up the night sky dragged dragons, slayed.

What I most remember was their applause.
They replied. They joined in. The joke was at
Themselves to see their maim stupidities.
Too young to observe such rubbed nerve ends craved,
Had I known, the gay fornications
Of the unsmiling skull – their predator.
I learn, with no war to frame that laughter
Which had the roiled feel of an ocean surface,
(Young men and women, countless and random,
Their one uniformity this shared life),
Like they because I praise myself only
In the revolutions of the mirror
I am the hero of the middle class
And will go down with jazz and moment
Like they, raized by the urn's compliment.

Christopher Logue

Be Not Too Hard

Be not too hard for life is short
And nothing is given to man;
Be not too hard when he is sold and bought
For he must manage as best he can;
Be not too hard when he gladly dies
Defending things he does not own;
Be not too hard when he tells lies
And if his heart is sometimes like a stone
Be not too hard – for soon he dies,
Often no wiser than he began;
Be not too hard for life is short
And nothing is given to man.

William Plomer

A Summer Storm

This is the voluntary patients' wing,
This is the lounge, and that old dear
Watching the storm is eighty-nine.
She was an actress once: she is one still.

Flash, flash! The lightning snapshots eagerly
Her simpering bloodless face. With drums,
Big drums, thunder explodes and roars
And shakes the world and us: it can't shake her.

'So many flashlight photographs,' she beams,
'The whole press must be here. Oh, what a house!
They want a speech. Oh thank you, thank you all!
You're all so kind, you will be glad to know

'My doctor says my arteries are like
A woman of fifty's. Yes, he thinks I'm wonderful,
I know you'll all be glad to know he says
That if I'm careful I'll outlive myself.'

And as the velvet curtain of the rain
Slowly descends, the obsolete crinkled face
Displaces all its map of criss-cross paths
And forms what is intended as a smile,

And the force of habit lifts a colourless claw,
An old hen's foot, to blow a kiss.
God help us all, is this what habit does?
Let us not act as *us*, and end like this.

Peter Porter

A Minor Lear

That big piece I've left for the sparrows,
Back you starlings, you've had your share.
That square of neat pink icing
Is for my calm dove – a threepenny cake
Doesn't go far among my courtiers.

I divided my substance. Yes, once
I kept exchequer of my crumbs,
I budgeted. The air was blurred with wings
When my subjects beat to my hand
To take their patrimony: I gave and I withheld.

Now my plants won't live. All's mutinous and new,
The city simmers, listen to the sun.
My youngest daughter runs an estate car.
The cost of living! A packet of cut bread
Used to feed a generation of such sneaks.

Down Pride – a man's not a king because
He's followed by his pensioners
To the top of the world. I go down in the lift
And am polite to Mr Morgan in his box.
The sky's got into my head: it's raining quails and death.

Stevie Smith

Tenuous and Precarious

Tenuous and Precarious
Were my guardians,
Precarious and Tenuous,
Two Romans.

My father was Hazardous,
Hazardous,
Dear old man,
Three Romans.

There was my brother Spurious,
Spurious Posthumous,
Spurious was spurious
Was four Romans.

My husband was Perfidious,
He was perfidious.
Five Romans.

Surreptitious, our son,
Was surreptitious,
He was six Romans.

Our cat Tedious
Still lives,
Count not Tedious
Yet.

My name is Finis,
Finis, Finis,
I am Finis,
Six, five, four, three, two,
One Roman,
Finis.

54

Bernard Spencer

The Rendezvous

I take the twist–about, empty street
– balconies and drapes of shadow
– and glimpse chalk slogans on each wall,
(now governments have done their work)
that the fanatic or the duped,
even children are taught to scrawl:
the patriotic, 'Tyrants', 'Vengeance',
'Death to', etc.

              Hooped
the barbed wire lies to left and right
since glass crashing, cars on fire,
since the mob howled loose that night,
gawky, rusty, useful wire
with little dirty fangs each way,
(what craftsman makes this fright?).
Black on that chemist's lighted window
steel helmets, rifle tops. I sense
the full moon wild upon my back
and count the weeks. Not long from this
the time we named comes round.

              And true
to loves love never thought of, here
with bayonet and with tearing fence,
with cry of crowds and doors slammed to,
waits the once known and dear, once chosen
city of our rendezvous.

Terence Tiller

Political Prisoner

They set him labouring, who meant
all strength of his to faint and kneel;
but he endured, because she leant
her own smooth body to the wheel.

They stripped him naked, and they bound
with holly-branches every limb:
sure comfort against cold and wound,
her nakedness lay over him.

They held away all food and drink
but poison, tempting him towards death:
how should his resolution sink,
who lived upon her touch and breath?

They tied a rat upon his breast
for torment, having not foreseen
to whose pain he must yield at last,
her own breast offered in between.

They took her from him, and the cell
they shut him in was dark and sour:
she *was*: and this dissolved the wall,
and lit a candle every hour.

They quarried selfhood from his skull,
humanity from flesh and face:
still she stole back to him, to call
the ruined house her dwelling-place.

1964

Thomas Blackburn

A Broken Image

Walking in the Alps, my wife and I
Found a broken cross, half buried under
A fall of rock and turf and red scree.

Since it came away, the figure
Of Christ, easily from its rusted
Nail, under a worm-eaten, weather

Worn image of wood we transported
From Italy without permission
We drink our wine now, eat our daily bread.

Since friends who come here often mention
The great skill of an anonymous
Carver of beech-wood, the conversation

Is enriched by his being with us
As at Cana, I'd say, if the bowed head
With any locality or surface

Chatter could be associated.
Leaning forward, as it does, from our wall
To where silence is concentrated

Outside and within the ephemeral
Constellations of energy,
Because it says nothing reasonable,

This image explains nothing away,
And just by gazing into darkness
Is able to mean more than words can say.

John Fuller

Buffalo

from *Landscapes of Western New York*

The metered tarmac elevates
Its clean technologies, distils
The whiff of chemicals, a mile
Of steel. And Erie shrugs the stains.

Far from the shore a city collapses
Into its suburbs: four-garage
Colonial, and shops for tartan.
Executives flop into pools.

Industry and avenue:
The civic idea pacifies
The furies. Winking boulevards
Offer a dangerous escape.

For tourists, curios and wreckers
Assert a kind of grammar, cars
Smooth past hotels coloured as cake,
A wilderness of lowered shades.

Warmed by the sobbing of the lights
We reach the core, a cut-price noon,
The taste of our solicitude,
The negro store, the golden dome.

Francis Hope

Dirty Bookshop

Rhubarb-pink buttocks jelly out above
    Black stocking-tops, white carpet, in *Bouquet*,
And next this vision kneels *Miss Modern Love*,
    Offering her nipples like a cocktail tray.

Art Poses shows a garden, neatly fenced
    With trellis which a naked Negress climbs;
Lusty and *Tease* glow dimly, propped against
    Flogging and Torture in Renaissance Times.

In one dark corner, dusty, creased, unbought,
    Printed in type less challenging than its name
Suggests, *The Sexual Side of Marriage* ought
    To put both stock and customers to shame.

In time, they say, we'll build a city where
    Nobody needs such grimy substitutes;
Where simultaneous climax fills the air
    And egoists freely couple with deaf mutes.

Till that harmonious day, better perhaps
    To bear down lightly, to let ill alone;
Even sympathy seems wrong ('Poor lonely chaps!').
    Let some pure alchemist cast his philosopher's stone.

Philip Larkin on

The Whitsun Weddings
(Faber & Faber) 1964

It would, perhaps, be fitting for me to return the heartening compliment paid by the selectors to *The Whitsun Weddings* with a detailed annotation of its contents. Unfortunately, however, once I have said that the poems were written in or near Hull, Yorkshire, with a succession of Royal Sovereign 2B pencils during the years 1955 to 1963, there seems little to add. I think in every instance the effect I was trying to get is clear enough. If sometimes I have failed, no marginal annotation will help now. Henceforth the poems belong to their readers, who will in due course pass judgment by either forgetting or remembering them.

If something must be said, it should be about the poems one writes not necessarily being the poems one wants to write. Some years ago I came to the conclusion that to write a poem was to construct a verbal device that would preserve an experience indefinitely by reproducing it in whoever read the poem. As a working definition, this satisfied me sufficiently to enable individual poems to be written. Insofar as it suggested that all one had to do was pick an experience and preserve it, however, it was much oversimplified. Nowadays nobody believes in 'poetic' subjects, any more than they believe in poetic diction. The longer one goes on, though, the more one feels that some subjects *are* more poetic than others, if only that poems about them get written whereas poems about other subjects don't. At first one tries to write poems about everything. Later on, one learns to distinguish somewhat, though one can still make enormously timewasting mistakes. The fact is that my working definition defines very little: it makes no reference to this necessary element of distinction, and it leaves the precise nature of the verbal pickling unexplained.

This means that most of the time one is engaged in

doing, or trying to do, something of which the value is doubtful and the mode of operation unclear. Can one feel entirely happy about this? The days when one could claim to be the priest of a mystery are gone: today mystery means either ignorance or hokum, neither fashionable qualities. Yet writing a poem is still not an act of the will. The distinction between subjects is not an act of the will. Whatever makes a poem successful is not an act of the will. In consequence, the poems that actually get written may seem trivial or unedifying, compared with those that don't. But the poems that get written, even if they do not please the will, evidently please that mysterious something that has to be pleased.

This is not to say that one is forever writing poems of which the will disapproves. What it does mean, however, is that there must be among the ingredients that go towards the writing of a poem a streak of curious self-gratification, almost impossible to describe except in some such terms, the presence of which tends to nullify any satisfaction the will might be feeling at a finished job. Without this element of self-interest, the theme, however worthy, can drift away and be forgotten. The situation is full of ambiguities. To write a poem is a pleasure: sometimes I deliberately let it compete in the open market, so to speak, with other spare-time activities, ostensibly on the grounds that if a poem isn't more entertaining to write than listening to records or going out it won't be entertaining to read. Yet doesn't this perhaps conceal a subconscious objection to writing? After all, how many of our pleasures really bear thinking about? Or is it just concealed laziness?

Whether one worries about this depends, really, on whether one is more interested in writing or in finding how poems are written. If the former, then such considerations become just another technical difficulty, like noisy neighbours or one's own character, parallel to a clergyman's doubts: one has to go on in spite of them. I suppose in raising them one is seeking some justification in the finished product for the sacrifices made on its behalf. Since it is the will that is the seeker, satisfaction is unlikely to be forthcoming. The only consolation in the whole business, as in just about every other, is that in all probability there was really no choice.

Peter Levi

Prometheus

The stone was granite: lichened, weathered, tough,
basalt too green, not natural enough,
limestone too silver, chalk too soft and bleak,
marble too lucid, sandstone brown and weak.
And he endured on that unwatered bed,
there the suns found him, and the vultures fed:
and pinned and fluttering on his breast of rock
he cried in recognition and in shock,
This is my own language, this is my place,
this vein and grain, this silent lichened face.

Peter Levi

Fragment from a Babylonian Epic

She set out into the land
towards their native village in darkness
those desolate houses where no one comes out,
the road has no turn, they stand lightless,
(they eat earth and dust, see no light,
sprout wings like birds) she saw confused
walls, bolted gates rusting unused.

James Reeves

A Sonata by Handel

I cranked my clockwork gramophone;
The music told me I should never tire
To hear its timeless tone.
It did not tell me and I did not care
What else might chance.
Older by thirty years and more,
I hear a different fiddle dance
And different fingers press the keys
To that consummate score.
All that was seen and unforeseen –
Wife, children, sickness, death and war,
The headlines of the time between –
Whatever it has taught, has taught me nothing
More than I knew before
Of that slow, rapid, rueful and euphoric dance
That periwigged blind German first performed
Than that it once was right, is right, and will be right
Whenever sounds excite
Whatever mind, whatever years elapse:
Such music is a view of life perhaps?

1965

Fleur Adcock

Think Before You Shoot

Look, children, the wood is full of tigers,
Scorching the bluebells with their breath.
You reach for guns. Will you preserve the flowers
At such cost? Will you prefer the death
Of prowling stripes to a mush of trampled stalks?
Through the eyes, then – do not spoil the head.
Tigers are easier to shoot than to like.
Sweet necrophiles, you only love them dead.

There now, you've got three – and with such fur, too,
Golden and warm and salty. Very good.
Don't expect them to forgive you, though.
There are plenty more of them. This is their wood
(And their bluebells, which you have now forgotten).
They've eaten all the squirrels. They want you,
And it's no excuse to say you're only children.
No one is on your side. What will you do?

Martin Bell

Running Mad

1

The moon is having her revenges,
Inventing girls like the moon.

A sharp blade
Sails the sky.

I saw her through glass, through glass.
No cancelling that out.

What is it that I have
To repent of or redress?

I bowed three times the next time, but
She was already a segment of melon.

2

I was stammering like a pundit,
At the back of the room appeared

A girl
Clear and radiant,

Piercing. I glanced. Stammered again
She went on shining, quietly.

Seamus Heaney

The Diviner

Cut from the green hedge a forked hazel stick
That he held tight by the arms of the V:
Circling the terrain, hunting the pluck
Of water, nervous, but professionally

Unfussed. The pluck came sharp as a sting.
The rod jerked down with precise convulsions,
Spring water suddenly broadcasting
Through a green aerial its secret stations.

The bystanders would ask to have a try.
He handed them the rod without a word.
It lay dead in their grasp till nonchalantly
He gripped expectant wrists. The hazel stirred.

Ted Hughes on

Ariel

by Sylvia Plath (Faber & Faber) 1965

In her earlier poems, Sylvia Plath composed very slowly, consulting her Thesaurus and Dictionary for almost every word, putting a slow, strong ring of ink around each word that attracted her. Her obsession with intricate rhyming and metrical schemes was part of the same process. Some of those early inventions of hers were almost perverse, with their bristling hurdles. But this is what she enjoyed. One of her most instinctive compulsions was to make patterns – vivid, bold, symmetrical patterns. She was fond of drawing – anything, a blade of grass, a tree, a stone, but preferably something complicated and chaotic, like a high heap of junk. On her paper this became inexorably ordered and powerful, like a marvellous piece of sculpture, and took on the look of her poems, everything clinging together like a family of living cells, where nothing can be alien or dead or arbitrary. The poems in *Ariel* are the fruits of that labour. In them, she controls one of the widest and most subtly discriminating vocabularies in the modern poetry of our language, and these are poems written for the most part at great speed, as she might take dictation, where she ignores metre and rhyme for rhythm and momentum, the flight of her ideas and music. The words in these odd-looking verses are not only charged with terrific heat, pressure and clairvoyant precision, they are all deeply related within any poem, acknowledging each other and calling to each other in deep harmonic designs. It is this musical, almost mathematical hidden law which gives these explosions their immovable finality.

Behind these poems there is a fierce and uncompromising nature. There is also a child desperately infatuated with the world. And there is a strange muse, bald, white and wild, in her 'hood of bone', floating over a landscape like that of the Primitive Painters, a burningly luminous vision of a Paradise. A Paradise which is at the same time eerily frightening, an unalterably spot-lit vision of death.

And behind them, too, is a long arduous preparation. She grew up in an atmosphere of tense intellectual competition and Germanic rigour. Her mother, first-generation American of Austrian stock, and her father, who was German-Polish, were both University teachers. Her father, whom she worshipped, died when she was nine, and thereafter her mother raised Sylvia and her brother single-handed. Whatever teaching methods were used, Sylvia was the perfect pupil: she did every lesson double. Her whole tremendous will was bent on excelling. Finally, she emerged like the survivor of an evolutionary ordeal: at no point could she let herself be negligent or inadequate. What she was most afraid of was that she might come to live outside her genius for love, which she also equated with courage, or 'guts', to use her word. This genius for love she certainly had, and not in the abstract. She didn't quite know how to manage it: it possessed her. It fastened her to cups, plants, creatures, vistas, people, in a steady ecstasy. As much of all that as she could, she hoarded into her poems, into those incredibly beautiful lines and hallucinatory evocations.

But the truly miraculous thing about her will remain the fact that in two years, while she was almost fully occupied with children and house-keeping, she underwent a poetic development that has hardly any equal on record, for suddenness and completeness. The birth of her first child seemed to start the process. All at once she could compose at top speed, and with her full weight. Her second child brought things a giant step forward. All the various voices of her gift came together, and for about six months, up to a day or two before her death, she wrote with the full power and music of her extraordinary nature.

Ariel is not easy poetry to criticize. It is not much like any other poetry. It is her. Everything she did was just like this, and this is just like her – but permanent.

Christopher Middleton

Old Bottles

It must have been long
I lay awake,
listening to the shouts
of children in the wood.
It was no trouble, to be awake;
not to know
if that was what I was.

But I had to buy
old bottles, barter
for steerage, candles too,
each stamped with my name.
It was hurry hurry
racing the factory canal toward
the town of the kangaroo.

Up the street I came
across a knot of dead boys.
In the room with a flying bird
on practising my notes
I found its lingo;
my body knew
those torsions of the cat.

She came by, that girl,
she said it's to you, to you
I tell what they are doing
in South Greece and Germany.
My parents killed, brother gone,
they read this letter, I'll
not be here, you do not understand.

In my striped pyjamas
I was not dressed for the journey.
I changed into padded zip
jacket, boots, canvas trousers,
my pockets bulged with the bottles,
I was carrying the candles,
and I ran and I ran.

Stevie Smith

V.

Adela is such a silly woman
Tom says Adela is going off her head

Adela is staying down in the country
She is v. happy

Dr Not is v. nice

Such a jolly old place quite like home

Dr Not is v. nice
Adela is v. happy

Adela is Not is
v.v. happy

With extensive grounds.

Stevie Smith

Yes, I know

That pale face stretches across the centuries
It is so subtle and yielding; yet innocent,
Her name is Lucretia Borgia.

Yes, I know. I knew her brother Cesare
Once. But only for a short time.

Ted Walker

Elegy for a Trotliner

I remember him. Even then,
when we were boys, he looked too worn
to weather out the season
of those winter afternoons
that rasped away the marram dunes.

He used to bring a ball of sun
to dribble from his fork's curled tines
and rinse away; already, often,
half a moon hung like a husk
from fingers of a tamarisk.

All the shingle, seeping, sang
with lives the sea had left the dusk;
intermittently bell-buoys rang
to smaller swells, more faintly, listing
one by one to breakers basting

them where they lay. Anxious, for
the last of his light was wasting,
he strode the souring foreshore.
Swiftly, before the rip-tide
turned, he dug firm sand that sighed

as he lifted it. He strung his line
of a hundred hooks beyond the braid
of matted wracks by the shine
of phosphor: swifter, snood by snood,
crouching, baited. And when he stood

calf-deep to sink the anchored tag,
there were November floes of cold
incising him, shells in the under-drag
to crampon his tread. It was his way
to walk towards the morning sky

75

and back by water's withdrawing hem
when there were gulls enough to see by.
Sometimes, walking early, I saw him
fling into a shallow box
the flapping catch he tore from the hooks.

I lie awake, cold nights like this,
and when his memory gently shakes
the moonlight through the frosting glass
to fill my room with gulls, the sound
of him will come as a less than wind:

the barren whistle that he left
blowing across the stones and sand
to a field where the linnets lift
over him, warm as he is now, deep
in the morning of his sleep.

1966

W. H. Auden

River Profile

Our body is a moulded river
                    Novalis

Out of a bellicose fore-time, thundering
head-on collisions of cloud and rock in an
up-thrust, crevasse-and-avalanche, troll country,
deadly to breathers,

it whelms into our picture below the melt-line,
where tarns lie frore under frowning cirques, goat-bell,
wind-breaker, fishing-rod, miner's-lamp country,
already at ease with

the mien and gestures that become its kindness,
in streams, still anonymous, still jumpable,
flows as it should through any declining country
in probing spirals.

Soon of a size to be named and the cause of
dirty in-fighting among rival agencies,
down a steep stair, penstock-and-turbine country,
it plunges ram-stam,

to foam through a wriggling gorge incised in softer
strata, hemmed between crags that nauntle heaven,
robber-baron, tow-rope, portage-way country,
nightmare of merchants.

Disembogueing from foothills, now in hushed meanders,
now in riffling braids, it vaunts across a senile
plain, well-entered, chateau-and-cider-press country,
its regal progress

77

gallanted for a while by quibbling poplars,
then by chimneys: led off to cool and launder
retort, steam-hammer, gasometer country,
it changes colour.

Polluted, bridged by girders, banked by concrete,
now it bisects a polyglot metropolis,
ticker-tape, taxi, brothel, foot-lights country,
à la mode always.

Broadening or burrowing to the moon's phases,
turbid with pulverized wastemantle, on through
flatter, duller, hotter, cotton-gin country
it scours, approaching

the tidal mark where it puts off majesty,
disintegrates, and through swamps of a delta,
punting-pole, fowling-piece, oyster-tongs country,
wearies to its final

act of surrender, effacement, atonement
in a huge amorphous aggregate, no cuddled
attractive child ever dreams of, non-country,
image of death as

a spherical dew-drop of life. Unlovely
monsters, our tales believe, can be translated
too, even as water, the selfless mother
of all especials.

George Barker

'The clock is banging'
from The Golden Chains, 4

The clock is banging
    on the wall
like that shape hanging
    over us all

whispering of things
    that come to pass
when bones have wings
    and flesh is grass.

Jack Clemo

Carmel

(to St Thérèse of Lisieux)

Gaunt as an ancient dungeon,
Those cloisters of Normandy:
The crucifix raked the unsown breast
Till a breaking lung threw up a blossom
Opening to storm and liberty.

You were the true child-bride,
Burning among the passionless, cold-eyed,
Uncomprehending species, bats or fish,
Who glided in corridors,
Clicked rosaries or tapped a refectory dish.

The chill bell ringing for compline,
Thin nuns' voices chanting in candlelight:
Through such bars of routine
The child-spouse cried of exile,
She-bird pining to match her eagle's flight.

Who are the cheated, who forfeit most?
Not you, Thérèse, but earth-drugged lovers,
Tricked by the unscarred chalice,
Breeding in ignorance of the white host.

Who, tasting the Word, yearns deepest
For the ultimate Carmel of the soul?
Not the frosted nun, but the doubly wedded,
Flesh-fertile pilgrims, canonized at Cana,
Struggling with hints of riper paradox;
Spirits still chaste for Christ, heaven's eagle,
Amid the bedded senses' shocks.

David Jones

A, a, a, Domine Deus

I said, Ah! what shall I write?
I enquired up and down.
                    (He's tricked me before
with his manifold lurking-places.)
I looked for His symbol at the door.
I have looked for a long while
                    at the textures and contours.
I have run a hand over the trivial intersections.
I have journeyed among the dead forms
causation projects from pillar to pylon.
I have tired the eyes of the mind
                    regarding the colours and lights.
I have felt for His Wounds
                    in nozzles and containers.
I have wondered for the automatic devices.
I have tested the inane patterns
                    without prejudice.
I have been on my guard
                    not to condemn the unfamiliar.
For it is easy to miss Him
                    at the turn of a civilization.
    I have watched the wheels go round in case I might see the
living creatures like the appearance of lamps, in case I might see
the Living God projected from the Machine. I have said to the
perfected steel, be my sister and for the glassy towers I thought I
felt some beginnings of His creature, but *A, a, a, Domine Deus*,
my hands found the glazed work unrefined and the terrible
crystal a stage-paste . . . *Eia, Domine Deus.*

Norman Nicholson

Have You Been to London?

'Have you been to London?'
My grandmother asked me.
                              'No.' –
China dogs on the mantelshelf,
Paper blinds at the window,
Three generations simmering on the bright black lead,
And a kettle filled to the neb,
Spilled over long ago.

I blew into the room, threw
My scholarship cap on the rack;
Wafted visitors up the flue
With the draught of my coming in –
Ready for Saturday's mint imperials,
Ready to read
The serial in *Titbits*, the evangelical
Tale in the parish magazine,
Under the green
Glare of the gas,
Under the stare of my grandmother's Queen.

My grandmother burnished her sleek steel hair –
Not a tooth in her jaw
Nor alphabet in her head,
Her spectacles lost before I was born,
Her lame leg stiff in the sofa corner,
Her wooden crutch at the steady:
'They shut doors after them
In London,' she said.

I crossed the hearth and thumped the door *to*;
Then turned to Saturday's stint,
My virtuosity of print
And grandmother's wonder:
Reading of throttler and curate,
Blood, hallelujahs and thunder,
While the generations boiled down to one
And the kettle burned dry
In a soon grandmotherless room;

Reading for forty years,
Till the print swirled out like a down-catch of soot
And the wind howled round
A world left cold and draughty,
Un-latched, un-done,
By all the little literate boys
Who hadn't been to London.

Brian Patten

Little Johnny's Final Letter

Mother,
    I won't be home this evening, so
    don't worry; don't hurry to report me missing.
    Don't drain the canals to find me,
    I've decided to stay alive, don't
    search the woods, I'm not hiding,
    simply gone to get myself classified.
    Don't leave my shreddies out,
    I've done with security.
    Don't circulate my photograph to society
    I have disguised myself as a man
    and am giving priority to obscurity.
    It suits me fine;
    I have taken off my short trousers
    and put on long ones, and
    now am going out into the city, so
    don't worry; don't hurry to report me missing.

    I've rented a room without any curtains
    and sit behind the windows growing cold,
    heard your plea on the radio this morning,
    you sounded sad and strangely old . . . .

Ruth Pitter

In the Open

Move into the clear.
Keep still, take your stand
Out in the place of fear
On the bare sand;

Where you have never been,
Where the small heart is chilled;
Where a small thing is seen,
And can be killed.

Under the open day,
So weak and so appalled,
Look up and try to say,
Here I am, for you called.

You must haunt the thin cover
By that awful place,
Till you can get it over
And look up into that face.

1968

R. S. Thomas on

Not That He Brought Flowers

(*Hart-Davis*) 1968

I am naturally pleased that the Poetry Book Society has made my book its Christmas choice. As this means that some eight hundred readers will receive a copy whether they want it or not, it is incumbent upon me to say something about these particular poems rather than about poetry in general.

I am a Welshman who has lived most of his life in Wales. I speak its language and know its problems, as well as its history and literature. These facts are responsible for some of the poems. As Welsh people form a very small proportion of the population of these islands, the appeal of such poems will be limited. A large majority of the people of the United Kingdom, Welsh or otherwise, is urban and participant in the scientific-technological revolution. Of what significance to them are the poetic statements of one who has deliberately kept to the back-waters of rural life, concerning himself with the things that are passing away? I am a priest of the Christian Church, another minority position, which will appear reactionary and functionless to most people. Yet all these facts about me have had some share in the production of the poems in this book.

I do not wish to isolate myself from my fellow poets. While each of us may be striving after some personal identity in his poetry, the difficulties of writing it are common to us all: the effort to marry the words and the tune; the struggle to keep the mind moving poetically; the concern to get right on paper what seemed right in the head; the task of avoiding propaganda, that is of exalting the message at the expense of the medium, or alternatively of perfecting the technique at the expense of the content.

Added to all this are the difficulties arising from the nature of contemporary society, transitional between the old one of the humanities and the new technological one.

A poet is traditionally the custodian of language, as well as its renewer. In the age of the computer and the mass media, the proliferation of terms, the commercial inflation of adjectives, the encroachment of the novelist, can he still sustain his role? I do not wish to generalize a personal failure of talent. When the genius appears, he does easily what had seemed impossible. The poet of the new age may already have been hatched in some incubator or other. For myself I cannot boast even a guitar. I play on a small pipe, a little aside from the main road. But thank you for listening.

1969

Donald Davie

To Helen Keller

Yours was the original freak-out: Samuel Beckett's
mutilated prodigies, for whose
sake these last years we bought so many tickets
and read so many books, were hotter news
when your and Anne Sullivan Macy's iron will.
back in the twenties, stooped to vaudeville.

One will, two persons . . . yes, let campus-rebels
account for education at that level,
that give, that take. I wonder if it troubles
our modish masters of sardonic revel
that you, who seemed typecast for it, were not
conscious of Black Comedy in the plot.

You were by force of circumstance, by force
of your afflictions, I suppose, the most
literary person ever was.
No sight nor sound for you was more than a ghost;
and yet because you called each phantom's name,
tame to your paddock chords and colours came.

This too, at this, the mind of our time is appalled.
The Gutenberg era, the era of rhyme, is over.
It's an end to the word-smith now, an end to the Skald,
an end to the erudite, elated rover
threading a fiord of words. Four-letter expletives
are all of that ocean's plankton that still lives.

You, who had not foreseen it, you endured it:
a life that is stripped, stripped down to the naked,
asking what ground it has, what has ensured it.
Your answer was: the language, for whose sake it
seemed worthwhile in Tuscumbia, Alabama,
month after month to grope and croak and stammer.

Douglas Dunn on

Terry Street
(Faber & Faber) 1969

Yeats wrote in a letter of reply to a young woman who had sent him poems: ' . . . one should love best what is nearest and most interwoven with one's life'. Although I have only just discovered this beautiful piece of advice in Hone's biography of Yeats, it is something that I think I have always known. Yeats was of course advising that girl to continue writing about her native Ireland, but with a Scotsman's effrontery and recklessness I choose to be blind to the real significance the advice should have for me. Scotland is what I most want to write about and what I am least able to. The only way I can try to describe the poetry I have written so far, and it is not really for me to do this, is to suggest that I have tried to understand the familiar and the ordinary.

This, I hope, is at least true of the poems I wrote in the second of the two years I lived in a terrace off Terry Street in Hull. It was never my intention that the poems be read as social or any other kind of protest, nor was I recommending Terry Street as a better because simpler way of life. My experience of the place made it impossible for me to want to do either of these things. The poems are not slum-pastorals.

Terry Street became for me a place of sad sanity. It was an alternative to the gaudy shams everywhere, a cave under a waterfall. But in thinking of Terry Street like this I was probably kidding myself into believing there could be a place not entirely of the age and yet handy enough to it for purposes of observation. Poverty makes men look foolish as well as their lives uncomfortable and I was no exception. I began to feel strange and lost, as though I was trying to inflict loneliness on myself, and I came to dislike Terry Street, and left it, although I still live in Hull. 'We free ourselves from obsession that we may be nothing. The last kiss is given to the void.'

Geoffrey Grigson

Academic Futures

*(Meditation of a cliché-spinning second-rate young Maggot
deep in the Dept. of English)*

Living, mused Maggot in the binding, is
A crawling, walking, coupling, then a creep.
In this shape, mused Maggot in his binding still,
I may not die. But swing in a draught of old flies,
Turned black, empty and dry. Old toms neuter
But neutered never – M. mused on – are put to sleep.
Among lambs, lambs, old bits of sheep.
Old bull whales, old bluff admirals red-veined,
Like old simple ratings, stitched in sails,
Are finally committed to the deep.

1970

Peter Redgrove

The Curiosity-Shop

It was a Borgia-pot, he told me,
A baby had been distilled alive into the pottery,
He recommended the cream, it would make a mess of anybody's face;
My grief moved down my cheeks in a slow mass like ointment.

Or there was this undine-vase, if you shook it
The spirit made a silvery tinkling inside;
Flat on the table, it slid so that it pointed always towards the sea.
A useful compass, he said.
I could never unseal this jar, tears would never stop flowing towards
the sea.

Impatiently he offered me the final item, a ghoul-sack,
I was to feed it with rats daily unless I had a great enemy
Could be persuaded to put his head inside;
That's the one! I said,
That's the sackcloth suit sewn for the likes of me
With my one love's grief, and my appetite for curiosity.

1971

Thom Gunn on

Moly

(Faber & Faber) 1971

Picture Odysseus, deep in thought, walking through a dense green wood on a lonely island. He walks slowly but directly toward the house of the witch Circe, whom he has never seen. Yet he knows that she has turned his sailors into pigs, and he has no idea how he is going to rescue them or even save himself from the same transformation. Suddenly Hermes appears before him, in the guise of a boy – for a boy here helps the man. He tells Odysseus of the full difficulties before him and then shows him a herb growing at his feet, which he calls Moly. By eating this herb, Odysseus will be proof against Circe's powers.

It is magic, but if magic transforms us or keeps us proof against transformation, then it enters everybody's life. Magic is not completely separate from ordinary processes: it works by strengthening or inhibiting an impulse in us, even if that impulse is something we didn't recognize as being there. We can all take on the features of pigs – or what humans interpret as those features – we all have in us the germs of the brutal, greedy, and dull. And we can all avoid becoming pigs, though to do so we must be wily and self-aware. Moly can help us to know our own potential for change: even though we are in the power of Circe or of time, we do not have to become pigs, we do not have to be unmanned, we are as free to make and unmake ourselves as we were at the age of ten.

Many a poet since Pound has liked to see himself as Odysseus, an explorer and adventurer who lives experience through, in detail, and yet can always extract himself from it. He is given to reflection, but as a moralist he is derivative. He is very lucky. He is aware of blood-powers and earth-powers that he does not fully understand, but they are sometimes very kind to him because he has recognized them and respected them. Their kindness most often takes the form of showing him the full range of possibilities when in a time of danger or despair there has seemed only one, and that a destructive one, available.

I am telling you how I see myself and how I see my book. It may be that this account of myself as a poet is only what I want to think. And there are certainly other ways of looking at my book. It could be seen as a debate between the passion for definition and the passion for flow, it could be seen as a history of San Francisco from 1965–1969, or as a personal memoir of myself during those years. But I think of it as being about Odysseus' meeting with Hermes, his eating of that herb, and his reflections on metamorphosis in the remaining walk he has before he reaches the thick stone-built house.

Michael Hamburger

The Glade

1

All day in the glare, on the salt lake's beaches,
All night in a fever, shaking.
That's done with. My travels are over.
Somehow I'm here: glade in a dense wood.
Leafage makes lace. The shadows are of it, in it,
The season is everymonth.
White sorrel around me, and white anemone,
Foxglove purple, strawberry red.
Apple shapes, pear shapes have lasted all winter.
And the snow gleams above dry moss.

You don't see it, you cannot see it, love,
Travelling still to a town the guidebook foretells:
How it is to have gone and returned and gone
And returned and forgotten to go
And forgotten the route and the place
And be there again, and be everywhere.

Stay with me, love, till my fingers have traced the landscape
On your body and into your mind.

2

May we lie there, you ask; and how long.
By the hour, for ever, on a bed leased
From the turning trees and the conifers.
Leaving again and again,
Again and again left
To the dark and the whorled light.

Can you bear the silence between us?
You're of it, love, you are in it.
I fondle the silence between us
When I touch you and when I have lost you.

So late, nothing can part us:
We belong to the glade.

Seamus Heaney

The Tollund Man

I

Some day I will go to Aarhus
To see his peat-brown head,
The mild pods of his eye-lids,
His pointed skin cap.

In the flat country nearby
Where they dug him out,
His last gruel of winter seeds
Caked in his stomach,

Naked except for
The cap, noose and girdle,
I will stand a long time.
Bridegroom to the goddess,

She tightened her torc on him
And opened her fen,
Those dark juices working
Him to a saint's kept body,

Trove of the turfcutters'
Honeycombed workings.
Now his stained face
Reposes at Aarhus.

II

I could risk blasphemy,
Consecrate the cauldron bog
Our holy ground and pray
Him to make germinate

The scattered, ambushed
Flesh of labourers,
Stockinged corpses
Laid out in the farmyards,

Telltale skin and teeth
Flecking the sleepers
Of four young brothers, trailed
For miles along the lines.

III

Something of his sad freedom
As he rode the tumbril
Should come to me, driving,
Saying the names

Tollund, Grauballe, Nebelgard,
Watching the pointing hands
Of country people,
Not knowing their tongue.

Out there in Jutland
In the old man-killing parishes
I will feel lost,
Unhappy and at home.

Kathleen Raine

For the Bride

I breathed the fragrance of the spray
My mother showed me: 'For the bride.'
'Where does the orange-blossom grow?'
'Not in this country,' she replied,
'But in that other elsewhere land
'Some call Spain, some Italy,
'Or in marbled orangeries
'Where upon branches ever green
'Snow thick with buds and opening flowers
'Hangs golden fruit the leaves below.'

An old lace curtain for a veil,
Crowned with hawthorn, lovely may,
White shells of newly opened flowers,
Heavy anthers ruby-red
Poised on filaments of gold,
A child all day in solemn play
The Bride no bride can ever be,
Yet knew the May Queen was not I,
That none has ever seen her face
Whom immemorial stories praise,
Bud, and leaf, and blossoming tree.

Modelled in plaster or in wax,
Behind a plate-glass window poised,
Her veil with synthetic garland wreathed
Aphrodite in her shrine
To whom the passing shop-girls pray
That each some day, one day may be
Beauty upon her bridal-day,
Whose form the image rectifies,
Sweet face and gentle fingers sheathed
Under coarse flesh and common clay.

She is the pang that wounds the heart,
Nuance of consciousness so fine,
Elusive recollection stirred
By scent of syringa in a park,
Or an old Hebridean song,
Lydian or myxolydian mode
A passing sweetness in the air,
Her still reflection in our dream
With orange or with myrtle crowned,
Whose sacred nuptials are elsewhere.

1972

Stewart Conn

Visiting Hour

In the pond of our new garden
were five orange stains, under
inches of ice. Weeks since anyone
had been there. Already by far
the most severe winter for years.
You broke the ice with a hammer.
I watched the goldfish appear,
blunt-nosed and delicately clear.

Since then so much has taken place
to distance us from what we were.
That it should come to this.
Unable to hide the horror
in my eyes, I stand helpless
by your bedside and can do no more
than wish it were simply a matter
of smashing the ice and giving you air.

1973

Charles Causley

The Whangbird

'Good gracious me,' the whangbird said,
'They told me all your kind were dead.
What brought you back from that cold bed?'
      A thread.

'Your face was made of curds and whey,
Your speech was black, your lip was grey.
Something went in your head, they say.'
      Away.

'You walked about with quavering tread,
Refused to eat your birthday spread,
Bit on a stone and called it bread.'
      Was fed.

'You followed every wind that blows
Through desert salt and seething snows.
What sharpened path was it you chose?'
      God knows.

'We can't forget how we were shown
The rough pit where your goods were thrown.
What thought sustained you there alone?'
      My own.

'Perhaps your weakness you'd have shed
If only you had gone and wed –
Look at young Harry, look at Fred . . . .'
      Looking, I said.

And looking at you, dear old thing,
Is that a canker on your wing,
And why do you no longer sing?
Why is your tongue so stale, and why
So limp and lustreless your eye,
And why do you no longer fly?

Furious, the whangbird stopped his spiel
And cried, 'If that's the way you feel –'
A last feather fell from his head.
'Not I! Not I!' he said.
                    And fled.

Charles Causley

Infant Song

Don't you love my baby, mam,
Lying in his little pram,

Polished all with water clean,
The finest baby ever seen?

Daughter, daughter, if I could
I'd love your baby as I should,

But why the suit of signal red,
The horns that grow out of his head,

Why does he burn with brimstone heat,
Have cloven hooves instead of feet,

Fishing hooks upon each hand,
The keenest tail that's in the land,

Pointed ears and teeth so stark
And eyes that flicker in the dark?

Don't you love my baby, mam?

Dearest, I do not think I can.
I do not, do not think I can.

Lawrence Durrell

Incognito

Outside us smoulder the great
World issues about which nothing
Can be done, at least by us two;
Inside, the smaller area of a life
Entrusted to us, as yet unendowed
Even by a plan for worship. Well,
If thrift should make her worldly ·
Remind her that time is boundless,
And for call-girls like business-men, money.

Redeem pleasure, then, with a proximate
Love – the other problems, like the ruins
Of man's estate, death of all goodness,
Lie entombed with me here in this
Oldfashioned but convincing deathbed.

Her darkness, her eye are both typical
Of a region long since plunged into
Historic ruin; yet disinherited, she doesn't care
Being perfect both as person and as thing.

All winter now I shall lie suffocating
Under the débris of this thought.

Tom Raworth

Philosophical Padding

we eat towards greatness
drive towards it
die towards it   that's the story of
that's the glory of
love

Tom Raworth

Just Because My Teeth Are Pearly

'never a dull moment' said the sun
'you keep coming back to me, with dreams
and time. i've lost count
of your visits. perhaps we should come to some arrangement
go out at night, walk in my reflected light
and write, cry, and always love
the company of women when they dance'

Tom Raworth

Not A Step Do I Stir Until That Cat's Back To Its Colour

civilization was pushing around aging molecules saying
'lovely . . . a new patch of lung' and 'aching doesn't thank'
when a sunbeam hit my son, throwing his tiny full colour reflectior
onto the centre of the flickering black and white screen

Vernon Scannell

The Loving Game

A quarter of a century ago
I hung the gloves up, knew I'd had enough
Of taking it and trying to dish it out,
Foxing them or slugging toe-to-toe;
Keen youngsters made the going a bit too rough;
The time had come to have my final bout.

I didn't run to fat though, kept in shape,
And seriously took up the loving game,
Grew moony, sighed, and even tried to sing,
Looked pretty snappy in my forty-drape.
I lost more than I won, earned little fame,
Was hurt much worse than in the other ring.

Stephen Spender

A Girl Who Has Drowned Herself Speaks

If only they hadn't shown that cruel mercy
Of dredging my drowned body from the river
That locked me in its peace, up to their surface
Of autopsy, and burial and forms –
This, which was my last wish, might have come true –
That when the waves had finally washed away
The remnants of my flesh, the skull would stay –
But change to crystal. Things outside
Which it had looked at once, would swim into
Eye sockets that looked at them: through
The scooped-out caverns of the skull, would dart
Solid phosphorescent fish, where there had been
Their simulacra only in the brain.

Eric W. White

Farewell to Stevie

The last time I saw you was in that stuffy church hall.
Each word you half spoke, half sang,
Dropped like a pebble
Into a quiet pool of silence,
Making a submarine cairn by accretion –
Your poem, your thing.
And the concentric ripples grew wider and wider,
Overlapping each other before dying away.

After the reading you came up to me with a reproachful
                                                    air.
– Eric, you were asleep!
– Stevie, I protest. I wasn't.
– I could see you at the end of the row. Your eyes were
                                                    closed.
– The better to listen. I heard every word.
– Your head nodded.
– In time with your A and M chanting.
– Darling, as I looked at you, I couldn't help thinking of
  those oysters.
– Ah! So you've not forgotten?
– What a luncheon party! Norah in that lovely red hat;
  Cecil looking like the Poet Laureate; and you ordering
  all those oysters, which took so long to arrive!
– It was maddening, Stevie, especially as you had such
  an appetite after the investiture.
– They offered no refreshment at the Palace, not even a
  glass of sherry.
– But you got your gold medal.

I still see the quick flick of your smile. But now,
Thinking of the frightened way it went out,
I wonder if you were really smiling at all.
They say that shortly afterwards,
As you lay speechless on your sick-bed,
You asked by signs for pencil and book, and firmly ringed
A word in one of your poems,
A ripple arrested –
'*Death*'.

1974

Joan Barton

Great House on View Day

Best of all, the attics, through whose high windows
swathes of light pour in
and old lawns roofed with cedars stretch away
to private woods,
parkland and private woods and private places,
and greenness reaching to infinity;

in dove-coloured miles of early morning rain
the far kok-kok of pheasants; silences
winding it round. Someone should be here
contentedly alone
writing their masterpieces
testing their verses on this private air.

A someone looking out: for looking in
discovers low-roofed warrens – servants' rooms:
two to each sagging bed,
iron frame and ancient flock, the flowered po,
the tin alarms
forever jumping in the dark cold head.

Patricia Beer

Prochorus Thompson

Notice Prochorus Thompson. He has won
A competition with the smallest bones
In the whole churchyard. And the man-size grave
He shares with none tops all the tombstones.

Three months of life two hundred years ago.
From harvest time to ailing in November
He came to nothing much, even that Christmas
Not much for anybody to remember.

But little Prochorus Thompson bides his time.
He is the right length for sightseers
Who pay no attention to the corpses
That lived for fifty, sixty speaking years.

Evergreen and rank are the paths between
The yew trees, and lichen creeps like evil
Over men who worked hard and dropped dead,
Women at menopause who saw the devil.

The balance of the churchyard must be righted.
May the full-grown dead seem interesting. May all
Children live longer than Prochorus Thompson.
Strangle the church tower and the passing bell.

Roy Fisher

On the Open Side

On the open side, look out
for sun-patches of sea-blue:

if you see them
it's beginning to shift
with factory towers along the edge,
chalk-white and silver,
empty even of machines

– the other life,
the endless other life,
endless beyond the beginning;

that holds and suddenly presents
a sunny day twenty years ago,
the open window of a train
held up on an embankment for an hour:

down the field there were children playing
round a concrete garage.
That was all. Something the other life wanted –
I hadn't kept it.

              But look out
for the sea-blue patches.
They'll not make problems.

Roy Fuller

Twenty Years of the Poetry Book Society

New Zealand House, Haymarket. Sixteenth floor.
The city's white and greys and sudden green
Fill all the vista to the arching blue.

Cruelly level at this chopper's height,
The February sun. It shines on poets
Invited for an anniversary drink

And makes the party like the last in Proust.
To see bent veins, thin hair, large corporations,
Almost cheers one about one's own decay.

Dear co-slaves of the Muse, I might, if pressed
(The mid-day boozing clearly starts to work),
Approve your various poetries *en bloc*.

Such funny shapes to seek the beautiful,
Such feeble minds to make a cogent form,
Such egotists to interpret life and nature!

Are all we present mutual friends – or foes?
And does the rest of England, in the end,
Not require beauty, shape or explication?

Doubtless some fellow poets eyeing my
Trousers of daring check, plus clipped moustache
(With other curious traits that I don't see),

Are thereby confirmed in their low estimate
Of what I write – being less full of scotch
And sentiment and years than now I am.

I can't help thinking how in each crazed head
This narrow craftsmen's world is broadened out –
Beyond the urban concrete to the fields;

Into the empyrean; and the past.

Roy Fuller

The Same After Twenty-Five Years

I.m. James Reeves 1909–78

That was the party, hearing a crash, I thought
Some awful bard (even a name occurred)
Was testing Martini's generosity

With overzealousness. One later heard
Old purblind Reeves had blundered soberly
Among the empty glasses. We talked anon –

Strangely enough had never met before –
He kindly, and I'd always written well
(For once) of him. So on the cruel sea

Two rusty vessels passed. And now it's gone,
That power – to enchant the child and say
Neat forms – that wished to be immortal; may

Prove so, for in the end posterity
Seems to like quite as much as death and passion
Mild loves and mishaps in its forebears' art.

As they move clear of back-scratching and fashion,
Some even on Martini's sixteenth floor,
Share the few victories of the human heart.

John Hewitt

The Mile Long Street

The mile long street you trudge to school,
past factory wall and painted sills,
house-doors, curtains, little shops,
that padlocked church with lettered board,
was staged and starred with asterisks.
First, harness-shop that flashed with brass,
bits, stirrups, bridles, whips and reins,
huge blinkers for shy animals,
round its door, the leather smells;
farther, under a large sign
which spelt that strange word Farrier,
an open gateway offered you
hammer on anvil, the sharp taste
of scorched horn hissing;
and, farther still, a narrow door,
with glint of straw, warm tang of hay,
scatter of grains fanned round the step
brought the flapping pigeons down.

If you were rich and had a mind
to buy yourself a little horse,
he could be saddled, shod and fed,
and never need to leave that street.

Molly Holden

In This Unremarkable Island

We are always surprised by our weathers.

A morning sky is calm and apparently settled.
We assume a fine day to come. But clouds,
fine and soft, and ruffed like a comma's wings,
appear like phantoms in the distant blue.
We pay them little attention – perhaps they are
only signs of September at its best, a mellow sun
and the grass thicker with dew and shadow
than in these last few months.

                              But I
know what they mean; I am not surprised
by our weathers because I have had, perforce,
to sit and watch them change and come and go,
over the church or the chestnut, for nine years now.
I know the patterns of the sky and what they portend!
So now I watch a faint dappling in the west appear,
without surprise, and then, from nowhere apparently,
smooth pale banks of long and elegant cloud
behind those ragged wings that seemed diaphanous
at first but now become solid and significant.
I know that there will follow clouds scaled and veined,
and mares' tails twisted like ferns by winds at
incredible heights, and of incredibly cold
crystal, to such a coil of pattern
that no Celtic silversmith could match,
for all his skill. All this to herald rain!

Now, are we not spoilt, to live with such skies?
Although, soon after them, the sheet of faceless cloud
will move in on us from the west, drop,
silently drizzle, I would not live otherwhere.

They do not have such skies even in Calabria.

Elizabeth Jennings

Celebration of Winter

Any voice is soprano in this air,
Every star is seeding, every tree
Is a sign of belonging or being free,
Of being strong in the Winter atmosphere.
Nobody hesitates here.

There are sounds and there are spaces.
Human creatures could have left long ago,
Birds are migrants except
For an owl which woos and lullabies the night.
We are only waiting for snow.
The wind has swept away the brooding Summer,
Or has it taken flight?
Nostalgias are null. Eyes are a taper alight.

And Winter reaches ahead, it stretches, it goes
Further than dark. A fountain is somewhere still.
What voice will come and fill
The emptiness of its no-longer overflows?
Any birth in Winter is hallowed by more
Than Advents or Bethlehems. The seas compose
Themselves perhaps for an Age of Ice, a shore
Where a child lifts a wave, where one gull chose
Not an inland cluster but broken wing and claw.
Any voice is sharpened upon this air
And if the sky sagged there would be more than one star to spare.

Philip Larkin

The Life With a Hole in It

When I throw back my head and howl
People (women mostly) say
But you've always done what you want,
You always get your own way
– A perfectly vile and foul
Inversion of all that's been.
What the old ratbags mean
Is I've never done what I don't.

So the shit in the shuttered château
Who does his five hundred words
Then parts out the rest of the day
Between bathing and booze and birds
Is far off as ever, but so
Is that spectacled schoolteaching sod
(Six kids, and the wife in pod,
And her parents coming to stay) . . .

Life is an immobile, locked,
Three-handed struggle between
Your wants, the world's for you, and (worse)
The unbeatable slow machine
That brings what you'll get. Blocked,
They strain round a hollow stasis
Of havings-to, fear, faces.
Days sift down it constantly. Years.

George MacBeth

An Ageing

There is an ageing in the height of tiles,
And in the balancing of simple spoons;
An ageing in the edges of old files,
And in the trembling substance of new tunes.

There is an ageing on the work of clubs,
And on the surfaces of gathered skins;
An ageing on the ground, that sifts and rubs,
And on the troubled air, that weighs and pins.

There is an ageing that descends and breaks,
And salts the vestiges it needs to clear;
An ageing that absorbs all that it shakes,
And is invisible, and coming near.

Nothing survives this ageing, nor its climb:
And nothing will, not even this last rhyme.

Norman MacCaig

Stars and Planets

Trees are cages for them: water holds its breath
To balance them without smudging on its delicate meniscus.
Children watch them playing in their heavenly playground;
Men use them to lug ships across oceans, through firths.

They seem so twinkle-still, but they never cease
Inventing new spaces and huge explosions
And migrating in mathematical tribes over
The steppes of space at their outrageous ease.

It's hard to think that the earth is one –
This poor sad bearer of wars and disasters
Rolls-Roycing round the sun with its load of gangsters,
Attended only by the loveless moon.

Roger McGough

Blazing Fruit

(or The Role of the Poet as Entertainer)

During dinner the table caught fire.
No one alluded to the fact
and we ate on, regardless of
the flames singeing our conversation.

Unaware of the smoke
and the butlers swooning,
topics ranged from Auden
to Zefferelli. I was losing
concentration however, and being
short on etiquette, became tense
and began to fidget with the melting cutlery.

I was fashioning a spoon
into a question mark
when the Chablis began to steam
and bubble. I stood up,
mumbled something about having left the gas running
and fled blushing
across the plush terrain of the carpet.

The tut-tut-tutting could be heard above
the cra-cra-cracking of the bone china.

Outside, I caught a cab
to the nearest bus stop.
While, back at the table,
they were toying with blazing fruit
and discussing the Role of the Poet as Entertainer,
when the roof fell in.

John Wain

Nuffield

(from a group of poems about Oxford)

Before he came, the country and the town
Had settled down to something like accord.
A river slow but deep enough to drown:
Roads, markets. Barns where harvest could be stored.

November coal-smoke, river-mist in June
Made one flat sea beneath the pigeon's flight.
Steeple and anvil rang to the one tune.
St Aldate's heard the foxes bark at night.

Against this treaty Nuffield launched his war:
His weapons progress, profits, trusts and banks:
His prizes sales, promotions, more, more, more:
The cars rolled through the streets like tinny tanks.

What did their Leader dream of? With what shapes
People the empty spaces of the sky?
Nymph radiator-caps? Satiric apes?
What made him laugh? And did he ever cry?

If so, at what? At losses, or at fears?
What would the sadness be, of such a mind?
Petrol and money dripped away his years:
What knowledge could he lose, what secret find?

He died. We live among the things he willed.
Concrete and tyres. Shrouded in pastoral names
(Rose Hill and Blackbird Leys) the world he killed
Mocks us. *Sick hurry and divided aims.*

1975

Michael Burn

Welsh Love Letter

Were all the peaks of Gwynedd
In one huge mountain piled,
Cnicht on Moelwyn,
Moel-y-gest, Moel Hebog,
And Eryri on top,
And all between us,
I'd climb them climb them
All!
To reach you.
O, how I love you!

Were all the streams of Gwynedd
In one great river joined,
Dwyfor, Dwyryd,
Glaslyn, Ogwen,
And Mawddach in flood,
And all between us,
I'd swim them swim them
All!
To reach you.
O, how I love you!

Were all the forts of Gwynedd
In one great fortress linked,
Caer and castle,
Cricieth, Harlech,
Conwy, Caernarfon,
And all in flames,
I'd jump them jump them
All!
To reach you.
O, how I love you!

See you Saturday,
If it's not raining.

D. J. Enright

Seaside Sensation

The strains of an elastic band
Waft softly o'er the sandy strand.
The maestro stretches out his hands
To bless the bandiest of bands.

Their instruments are big and heavy –
A glockenspiel for spieling Glock,
A handsome, bandsome cuckoo clock
For use in Strauss (Johann not Lévi),

Deep-throated timpani in rows
For symphonies by Berlioz,
And lutes and flutes and concertinas,
Serpents, shawms and ocarinas.

The sun is shining, there are miles
Of peeling skin and healing smiles.
Also water which is doing
What it ought to, fro- and to-ing.

But can the band the bandstand stand?
Or can the bandstand stand the band?
The sand, the sand, it cannot stand
The strain of bandstand and a band!

Now swallowed up are band and stand
And smiling faces black and tanned.
The sand was quick and they were slow.
You hear them playing on below.

Seamus Heaney on

North

(Faber & Faber) 1975

Perhaps the first function of a poem is to assuage the poet's need for it to exist. For a while I found my needs satisfying themselves in images drawn from Anglo-Saxon kennings, Icelandic sagas, Viking excavations, and Danish and Irish bogs, and the result is the bulk of the poems in the first section of *North*. The second section is the result of a need to be explicit about pressures and prejudices watermarked into the psyche of anyone born and bred in Northern Ireland.

The title of the book, therefore, gestures towards the north of Ireland and the north of Europe. The first poems are set in Mossbawn, my earliest home, the last one in Wicklow, where I moved in 1972. Both place names have Norse elements. In fact, the language and landscape of Ireland, as the poem set on the archaeological site at Belderg insinuates, can be regarded as information retrieval systems for their own history: the bog bank is a memory bank.

The word 'bog' itself is one of the few borrowings in English from the Irish language. It means 'soft' in Irish, soft and wet, and one of its usages survives in the Hiberno-English expression, 'A soft day'. But in our part of the country we called the bog the 'moss', a word with Norse origins probably carried there by the Scots planters in the early seventeenth century. So in the bog/moss syndrome, one can diagnose a past of invasion, colonization and language shift, a past which, as Seamus Deane has pointed out, 'the Irish are conscious of as a process which is evidently unfulfilled'.

I cannot say why I should be possessed by past, language and landscape, but many of the poems wrought themselves out of that nexus; as Robert Frost put it, 'a poem begins as a lump in the throat, a homesickness, a lovesickness. It finds the thought and the thought finds the words.'

During the last few years there has been considerable expectation that poets from Northern Ireland should 'say' something about 'the situation', but in the end they will only be worth listening to if they are saying something about and to themselves. The truest poetry may be the most feigning but there are contexts, and Northern Ireland is one of them, where to feign a passion is as reprehensible as to feign its absence.

John Heath-Stubbs

Send for Lord Timothy

The Squire is in his library. He is rather worried.
Lady Constance has been found stabbed in the locked
                                Blue Room, clutching in her hand
A fragment of an Egyptian papyrus. His degenerate half-brother
Is on his way back from New South Wales.
And what was the butler, Glubb,
Doing in the neolithic stone-circle
Up there on the hill, known to the local rustics
From time immemorial as the Nine Lillywhite Boys?
The Vicar is curiously learned
In Renaissance toxicology. A greenish Hottentot,
Armed with a knobkerry, is concealed in the laurel bushes.

Mother Mary Tiresias is in her parlour.
She is rather worried. Sister Mary Josephus
Has been found suffocated in the scriptorium,
Clutching in her hand a somewhat unspeakable
Central American fetish. Why was the little novice,
Sister Agnes, suddenly struck speechless
Walking in the herbarium? The chaplain, Fr O'Goose
Is almost too profoundly read
In the darker aspects of fourth-century neo-Platonism.
An Eskimo, armed with a harpoon
Is lurking in the organ loft.

The Warden of St Phenol's is in his study.
He is rather worried. Professor Ostracoderm
Has been found strangled on one of the Gothic turrets,
Clutching in his hand a patchouli-scented
Lady's chiffon handkerchief.
The brilliant under-graduate they unjustly sent down
Has transmitted an obscure message in Greek elegiacs
All the way from Tashkent. Whom was the Domestic Bursar
Planning to meet in that evil smelling
Riverside tavern? Why was the Senior Fellow,
Old Doctor Mousebracket, locked in among the incunabula?
An aboriginal Philipino pygmy,
Armed with a blow-pipe and poisoned darts, is hiding behind
The statue of Pallas Athene.

A dark cloud of suspicion broods over all. But even now
Lord Timothy Pratincole (the chinless wonder
With a brain like Leonardo's) or Chief Inspector Palefox
(Although a policeman, patently a gentleman,
And with a First in Greats) or that eccentric scholar,
Monsignor Monstrance, alights from the chuffing train,
Has booked a room at the local hostelry
(*The Dragon of Wantley*) and is chatting up Mine Host,
Entirely democratically, noting down
Local rumours and folk-lore.

Now read on. The murderer will be unmasked,
The cloud of guilt dispersed, the church clock stuck at three,
And the year always
Nineteen twenty or thirty something,
Honey for tea, and nothing
Will ever really happen again.

Charles Tomlinson

In the Intensity of Final Light

In the intensity of final light
    Deepening, dyeing, moss on the tree-trunks
Glares more green than the foliage they bear:
    Hills, then, have a way of taking fire
To themselves as though they meant to hold
    In a perpetuity of umber, amber, gold
Those forms that, by the unstable light of day,
    Refuse all final outline, drift
From a dew-cold blue into green-shot grey:
    In the intensity of final light
A time of loomings, then a chime of lapses
    Failing from woodslopes, summits, sky,
Leaving, for the moonrise to untarnish,
    Hazed airy fastnesses where the last rays vanish.

David Wright

The Musician

In the south aisle of the abbey at Hexham
I turned to make a remark on its Roman
Tomb; but she did not hear me, for the organ
Was playing in the loft above the rood-screen,
Laying down tones of bronze and gold, a burden
Of praise-notes, fingerings of a musician
There at the keys, a boy, his master by him,
Whose invisible sound absorbed my saying.

Music inaudible to me, barbarian,
But legible. I read in my companion
Its elation written in her elation.
'He is so young he can be only learning,
You would not have expected to hear such playing.
It's like a return to civilization.'
Unable to hear, able to imagine
Chords pondering decline, and then upwelling

There in that deliberate enclave of stone,
I remembered music was its tradition;
Its builder, Acca, taught by one Maban
To sing; who may have been the god of song,
Mabon the god of music and the young;
That another bishop of this church, St John,
Taught here a dumb man speech, says Bede; became
Patron and intercessor of deaf men.

1977

Elizabeth Bartlett

Surgery

On my desk lies an informative leaflet about lassa fever,
And also a note on which is scrawled *Can the doctor come.*
Mum is poorly again, and oblige, yours truly. P.S.
Can't phone, box not working. My phone rings,
And *nocte*, I write, *two tabs, mare 1 tab, 10 mg,*
And answer the call at the same time. If I sound distant,
So does she – South Africa maybe, bleeding in Soweto,
But no, she has a sort of headache, and no, she cannot
Come this morning, because she's having her hair done.
Tonight perhaps, when the whole circus starts again,
The lion roars, the clown feigns dead, the tent
Shudders in the wind, the patients applaud.

The post is waiting to disgorge a message of hope
At last destroyed, an X-ray form with a fatal shadow,
Or N.A.D., those divine initials to say there's nothing wrong,
No abnormality detected. Before I have time to remember
The warm bed I left an hour ago, from a mystical erotic dream
I only half recall, the surgery begins in earnest.
Some cough, some limp, some sit and gaze, and one small child
Runs in and out, so plump of cheek, red of lip, blue of eye,
And full of energy, he removes the S-TI ticket
From my Caligari filing-cabinet. If he were taller
Would he snatch the A–BA with his neat questing squirrel paws
Indifferent to where he is? He might, but half way through
The morning and half way through the post, I tear up a few
Drug company ads. Maybe I've ditched a miracle drug, or
Another thalidomide. Who knows?

I have unpacked the vaccines, and laid out the syringes,
And listed the house-calls, street by street, house by house,
When I see him standing at the door, gaunt and dignified,
Wearing a look of such suffering that even the squirrel
Runs to his mother and buries his face in her trousered lap.
He is a terminal case, and knows it, but he comes each week,
And for a moment, detachment deserts me. I want to cry,
Come here, my love, and I will save you. I will kiss and comfort
You, and bring you strawberries out of season, and wine
In a silver goblet, and deliver you from all pain and sorrow.
Come into the dream I left before I came this morning,
Briskly unlocking the door on another day, another surgery.

W. S. Graham

The Coastguard's Poem

1

On Gurnard's Head at two a.m.
I sit beside my shielded lamp
Guarding the coast against the stray
Port and star boards of the world.
My wife is asleep a mile away.

Windforce eight to ten
Gusting up the Beaufort Scale.
Visibility Nil, even if I went
Outside to wipe the salt sticking
Onto the glass. Can you hear me?

I write this down in red ink at
The end of the book and eat my piece.
The logbook is a book of stories
And handwritings of coastguards gone,
Logging faded catastrophes.

I hear the plates riveted
In Glasgow or Zanzibar
Grinding on the Gurnard's nose.
Remember me to the donkey-man
I carried up with streaming clothes.

I am the brain of Gurnard's Head
With my oil-lamp turned down
Guarding the vessels from the night
Gurnard up to Zennor Head
And all the rocks of their delight.

Two short. One long. Two short. One long.
You are standing in to danger.
And through the salt glass I see us
Fighting to save our souls. I hear
The roar of the great Celtic approaches.

2

Six o'clock on Gurnard's Head.
I've puffed out the lamp to let
The first beginning of the blue
Morning understand me again.
The sea-light is at the window.

My watch is ending now. Visibility
One mile. Windforce six to seven.
I see the white slow-motion spray
Shoot up from the Gurnard's nose.
My wife is asleep a mile away.

Thom Gunn

A Waking Dream

They are massing at the bank
on the slippery mud, the only light
leaking from the world behind them.
In the middle of the crowd
not in the front pushing but not laggard
on his way to the grey river,
one figure catches my eye.
I see in a strong glint of light
a thick neck half curtained
by black hair, and the back of a head
that I dare recognize,
though knowing it could be another's.
Fearfully, 'Tony!' I call.
And the head turns: it is indeed his,
but he looks through me and beyond me,
he cannot see who spoke,
he is working out a different fate.

Ted Hughes

A Memory

Your bony white bowed back, in a singlet,
Powerful as a horse,
Bowed over an upturned sheep
Shearing under the East chill through-door draught
In the cave-dark barn, sweating and freezing –
Flame-crimson face, drum-guttural African curses
As you bundled the sheep
Like tying some oversize, overweight, spilling bale
Through its adjustments of position

The attached cigarette, bent at its glow
Preserving its pride of ash
Through all your suddenly savage, suddenly gentle
Masterings of the animal

You were like a collier, a face-worker
In a dark hole of obstacle
Heedless of your own surfaces
Inching by main strength into the solid hour,
Bald, arch-wrinkled, weathered dome bowed
Over your cigarette comfort

Till you stretched erect through a groan
Letting a peeled sheep leap free

Then nipped the bud of stub from your lips
And with glove-huge, grease-glistening carefulness
Lit another at it

Tom Paulin

Hidden Face

Her evenings are silk, a gentleness;
but the hot afternoons when her mother
bargains in the dusty market
for those two red saris that mean
she'll be married soon,
dry away her belief
in the boy she'll belong to.

The women crouch by the fire.
The sweet bitterness of the smoke blinds them
and each chappatti burns their fingers.
The pump clanks
and draws a pure water from the tubewell –
now the men bath
like patriarchs in the wide tank.
She serves them yoghurt in brass dishes.

When lights come on in the village
and a servant pads across the courtyard
to close the gates,
she walks softly on the flat roof
and gazes into a warm darkness
that might hide a face she's never seen.

If she could only walk out to meet him,
This lover who shares her sadness.

Peter Reading

Early Morning Call

At three this morning there is light enough to see
that the steam squeezed from this pasture and the
mist veiling holiday mornings when you were a boy
are no different; curlews employ
the same diatonic now as then. No, the difference is
    that the same phenomena don't have the same impact.
It is chilling to suddenly grasp the very simple fact
that you do not feel as *well* as then,
nor, you may be sure, ever will again.

Anne Stevenson

Blind Man and Child

'He can't see anything at all'
woke her amazement.
'Then you can't see me?'
                              'No.'
'Or the green grass, or the road,
that tree?'
                              'No.'
'Then what do you see?
Darkness?'
                              'Darkness mainly.'

'Do you remember
what you used to see?'
                              'I remember.'

She took his hand.
'Then come with me.
I'll do the seeing.
Maybe then you'll dream
just what it ought to be.'

They came to steer her from him
in case he was cross.
But no, she had no pity.

He was weighted with her like a cause.

Hugo Williams

Model Girl

Arching perfectly plucked eyebrows
Over blue eggshell eyes
She tells me it is possible in her country
To go all the way
From Viipuri on the Gulf of Finland
To Jisalmi, far inland,
On little steamers
Which thread through channels in the rocks
And forested islands.
Moving her hand through the air
She describes how certain rivers and lakes
Cascade into other lakes
In magnificent waterfalls
Which provide all the electricity for Finland.

Kit Wright

My Version

I hear that since you left me
Things go from bad to worse,
That the Good Lord, quite rightly,
Has set a signal curse

On you, your house and lover.
(I learn, moreover, he
Proves twice as screwed-up, selfish
And sodden, dear, as me.)

They say your days are tasteless,
Flattened, disjointed, thinned.
Across the waste my absence,
Love's skeleton, has grinned.

Perfect. I trust my sources
Of information are sound?
Or is it just some worthless rumour
I've been spreading round?

1978

Peter Porter on

The Cost of Seriousness

(Oxford University Press) 1978

A writer finds some of his works more difficult to introduce than others, and as I have had poems chosen by the Poetry Book Society before, I trust that subscribers will excuse my offering a shorter-than-usual prefatory piece. Perhaps I should try to explain the title. I chose it (it is a poem title also, of course) because it seemed to me to describe the book's main concern, which is with the inability of art (poetry in this case) to alter human circumstances or alleviate human distress. I think such a point needs making in an age when we are being urged to produce ever more urgent and extreme forms of art. After Auschwitz, they say, all art must be existential and at the edge of desperation. I am sure that the opposite is the case. It is the duty of art to make palatable somehow the real tragedy of the world. It must tell the truth about the facts of that tragedy at the same time. This is a tall order but one which poets have to face up to. One way of doing so, I believe, is to question the machinery of language, to try to test the worth of the words we use to describe our feelings. I don't mean games with words but a constant awareness of the shapes language makes of itself. Such questioning means that poetry can never hope to be very popular. Yet its feelings should be universal.

To come to the particular: most of the poems in this book were written after the sudden and tragic death of my wife at the end of 1974. The grief is personal, but I hope the poems communicate to other people, and say something more than just regret. Those about my wife – 'An Angel in Blythburgh Church', 'An Exequy', 'The Delegate', 'The Easiest Room in Hell', and 'Evensong' – share the centre of the book with the 'Three Transportations', attempts to settle the empty continent of Australia with notable examples of the European and the American imaginations. The frame around them is made

143

of poems about England, Australia and the arts of litera-
ture, music and painting. There is an attempt at the end to
look forward to a renewal of life. The title poem asks
whether our emotions can be notated properly in words,
and the poem about the Renaissance painter Melozzo da
Forli asserts (but not too sadly) that art is 'only a language
of gestures'. But the shape of the gestures counts, and I
hope some of the shapes in my book make sense to their
readers, and look as if they'll last a while.

C. H. Sisson

The Skull and Cross-bones

The boy is strenuous, and possesses
  His limbs in hopes and promises;
The young man, when he pauses, seeks to lie
  So that the needle threads the eye.
It is one world, one flesh, and not his own.
  The true meaning of 'spirit' is 'alone',
So that is what he is; but so is she,
  And out of world and flesh, confusedly,
Come other spirits, like hunters from a wood,
  One after one, a group, they look.
Nature has wrinkled her brow; his own is clouded
  And the word that issues is said aloud.
It is in this way that the world is peopled.
  What savagery! We are better asleep,
Dreaming of wizards and the extreme edges
  Of the unmagical circle, and the wet sedges
Beyond which is the kingdom of the dead.
  Where does it lead to, when all is said?
Having gone round the world to no purpose,
  The old man sits and broods on the whole circus.
He has visited the female body, and the Spice Islands,
  Now he sits here in silence
Except for the croaking of his own body,
  Here a discomfort, there he is uneasy.
Nothing to call out for, the world is flat.
  There is an end of him, when you get to that.

Charles Tomlinson on

Selected Poems 1951–1974

(Oxford University Press) 1978

In putting together a selected poems that spans well over twenty years of writing, one re-experiences to a certain extent some of the tensions that went into the making of the various collections. Perhaps even more acutely there comes back to the mind the challenge of those moments – or rather months, and sometimes years – of transition between one book and another. Factors that made the transitions possible, fears and silences that threatened them – these are the presences that rise up once more.

I have tried in assembling this choice of my work to include those pieces which for me were essential to this process of poetic growth. Thus, though I was willing to sacrifice virtually the whole of my first pamphlet, *Relations and Contraries* of 1951, it contained a poem, 'Wakening with the Window over Fields', written in 1948, which I kept. This was the first poem of mine where I seemed to hear a world beyond myself that defined its existence in terms of a syncopated melody (thus pulling away from traditional metric) and also in terms of space, light and air. I knew now what I wanted to do, though I did not know how to do it.

In those days the airwaves seemed to be filled with the voice of Dylan Thomas, and the problem for a young poet – at least for *this* young poet – was to get beyond it towards something a little less lush. A step in this direction was made possible by the discovery of those poems of Wallace Stevens like 'Thirteen Ways of Looking at a Blackbird' – poems written in discrete fragments that permitted you to be true to immediate sensations without transforming them into grand opera. A little book, *The Necklace* of 1955, got me from 'Wakening with the Window over Fields' to its final poem, 'Fiascherino', where the fragments of sensation seemed to knit up into a more organic whole. This new unity came about because I had started to consider syntax, and it was precisely this –

146

meditating the relation between the shapes of sentences and the way we perceive things – that broadened the style invented in *The Necklace* and helped me write my first full-scale book, *Seeing is Believing* (1960).

It is not my intention here to map an entire poetic process, but to point out one or two saliences. Often a poem proves to be more of a bridge than one could have imagined at the time of its composition. From *The Way of a World* (1969) I began writing poems about politics and history – in *The Shaft* (1978), a recent PBS recommendation, there is, for instance, a sequence of poems about the French Revolution. I have retained in my *Selected Poems* a piece conceived when I was writing *The Necklace* in Italy in 1952, though not actually written until the early sixties. This poem, which appeared in *A Peopled Landscape* (1963), is called 'Up at La Serra'. As a poem, it is not perhaps entirely mature, but it represents my first attempt to grapple with a situation in which history has closed off alternatives and brought the protagonist to a pitch of crisis. Written so long ago, it seems to underlie many more recent poems such as 'Charlotte Corday' and 'For Danton' in *The Shaft* and, in the present selection, 'Prometheus', 'Assassin' and, in a rather different way, 'At Stoke'. But I must leave the reader to trace these continuities for himself, and trust that they are evidence not merely of personal concerns, but of general human ones.

1979

George Mackay Brown

A Man Between Two Hills: Culloden

Where are you going from here, man?
I have a small free place at the shore.

What will you do after this day?
Be silent and hidden and poor.

Where are your friends tonight?
I left some tarrying on the moor.

What of your king waiting in France for news?
He listens. Fiddles are stroked, a modish heart-piercing air.

When will you rouse you, a stag, again?
When I hear the small knock of a girl at the door.

What cry in the mountains then?
Men seeking still the wolf's and the wildcat's lair.

Ted Hughes

You Hated Spain

                   Spain frightened you. Spain
Where I felt at home. The blood-raw light,
The oiled anchovy faces, the African
Black edges to everything, frightened you.
Your schooling had somehow neglected Spain.
The wrought-iron grille, death and the Arab drum.
You did not know the language, your soul was empty
Of the signs, and the welding light
Made your blood shrivel. Bosch
Held out a spidery hand and you took it
Timidly, a bobby-sox American.
You saw right down to the Goya funeral grin
And recognized it, and recoiled
As your poems winced into chill, as your panic
Clutched back towards college America.
So we sat as tourists at the bullfight
Watching bewildered bulls awkwardly butchered,
Seeing the grey-faced matador, at the barrier
Just below us, straightening his bent sword
And vomiting with fear. And the horn
That hid itself inside the blowfly belly
Of the toppled picador punctured
What was waiting for you. Spain
Was the land of your dreams: the dust-red cadaver
You dared not wake with, the puckering amputations
No literature course had glamourized.
The juju land behind your African lips.
Spain was what you tried to wake up from
And could not. I see you, in moonlight,
Walking the empty wharf at Alicante
Like a soul waiting for the ferry,
A new soul, still not understanding,
Thinking it is still your honeymoon
In the happy world, with your whole life waiting,
Happy, and all your poems still to be found.

149

Michael Longley

View

I have put my arms around her skeleton
For fear that her forearms might unravel
Like hawsers, ligaments stiffening to kelp
That keeps ocean and boulders in their places,
Weights on the heart, ballast for the ribcage,
Stones to be lifted out of the currach
And arranged as a sundial where she points
To the same cottage on every island –
There's always a view over her shoulder.

Derek Mahon on

Poems 1962–1978

(Oxford University Press) 1979

My *Poems 1962–1978* constitute a sort of 'selected collected' edition, and no doubt their appearance in this form is premature and presumptuous. More distinguished poets than I have yet to take such a step – implying, as it does, a measure of finality, a canonical repose. But this is not really the case. A mere thirty-eight, I think of this volume not as a culmination – and what a slim achievement that would be! – but rather as, in some sense, a first book, the kind of thing you put behind you before proceeding to the real business of learning and trying to create. Most of these poems have appeared before in earlier collections – 'Night-Crossing', 'Lives', 'The Snow Party' – and a number of more recent or previously uncollected poems have been added, although the order is not strictly chronological. I've taken the opportunity of making a few revisions, which annoyed some of my friends; but let them reserve their annoyance, I say, for a future occasion, when I'll probably make yet more. No poem, somebody said, is ever finished. Indeed, even with the page proofs beside me, I can see revisions crying out to be made to the more *recent* poems; but it's too late, the book has gone to press.

One of the more recent poems, an attempted translation from the French of Jaccottet which I've called 'Ignorance' (*L'Ignorant* in the original), begins with the line, 'The older I get the more ignorant I become'. The original reads, '*Plus je vieillis et plus je croîs en ignorance*' – 'The older I get the more I *grow* in ignorance'. My own version tries to get the line into natural, conversational English, and the 'grow' is lost, though I think recovered in the course of the poem by other means. In any case, this 'growing in ignorance' is what I'm getting at. Having published my 'selected collected' (what used to be called, in a fine funerary phrase, 'all that I wish to preserve' up to the present), I feel myself released, or

151

partly, from the impertinent rhetoricism of what I suppose I must now regard as my 'early work', and at last in a position to *begin*. Jaccottet's 'growth in ignorance', after all, has much in common with Keats's 'negative capability'. *Poems 1962–1978* is the work of a young man who thought he knew quite a lot about one thing and another – a most unpoetical attitude – and discovered that he knew, in fact, nothing of importance. It was a painful discovery, but inevitable and, I hope, fruitful. Now, perhaps, he can begin to think about writing something really worthwhile, if at all. Watch this space.

Paul Muldoon

The One Desire

The palm-house in Belfast's Botanic Gardens
Was built before Kew
In the spirit that means to outdo
The modern by the more modern,

That iron be beaten, and glass
Bent to our will,
That heaven be brought closer still
And we converse with the angels.

The palm-house has now run to seed;
Rusting girders, a missing pane
Through which some delicate tree
Led by kindly light
Would seem at last to have broken through.
We have excelled ourselves again.

Craig Raine on

A Martian Sends a Postcard Home

(Oxford University Press) 1979

In spite of their evident variety, these poems have one thing in common. They were written after the birth of my daughter – a happy event, but one which, to my mind, accounts for the sombre overall tone. Few things bring mortality so vividly close as holding a perfect, vulnerable scrap of flesh in your arms. Especially if you happen also to be a heavy smoker. There is one poem, 'Sexual Couplets', which is intended as a *jeu d'esprit*, but I would be disappointed if this was seized on by those critics who persist in describing my work as dandified. Wit is not incompatible with seriousness: when Donne writes, in *The First Anniversarie*, 'How witty's ruine!', he means inventiveness, not facetiousness. Equally, I don't regard the use of metaphor and simile as unnatural or arty – either in Shakespeare's plays, ordinary conversation, or my own poetry. The equation (fashionable in the 60's) between sincerity and what Joyce called, as he repudiated it, 'a scrupulous meanness' of style now seems narrowly prescriptive: too often, unforced directness of expression declined into mere mannerism, widely copied because easily reproduced.

England has a tradition that emphasises the role of tone in poetry and rightly so. All the same, this frequently degenerates into something resembling caricature – a self-presentation that toadies to the reader and traps the writer, who introduces himself into his poems as unfailingly sensitive, modestly touched by venial guilt, but invariably charming. Berryman broke through this politesse by using himself as an anti-hero *in extremis*. I have deliberately chosen a neutral, objective tone which allows the images to speak for themselves – under authorial supervision, of course, but without overt moralising. I hope no one will be stupid enough to mistake this tone for lack of feeling.

Many critics are impressed by technical virtuosity – by

which they mean the dead perfection of the sestina and other futile fifteen-finger exercises. The couplet I use is essentially a flexible instrument capable of accommodating a huge variety of subject matter. The sestina strikes me as the poetic equivalent of an instrument for removing Beluga caviar from horses' hooves – bizarrely impressive, but finally useless. The unrhymed couplet, on the other hand, is more like the tin-opener – so useful that one is inclined to overlook its cleverness.

Carol Rumens

Almost in Walking Distance

Two centuries ago they would have taken
this same short cut through the farm,
the rough, scrubbed boys and girls to whom
corn-fields were work-a-day. In tight best boots
for the Sabbath, laughing tumbled country vowels,
on mornings blue and full of bells as this one,
they would have skirted the plait-haired rows
all the way to the crumbly lanes of Chaldon
and the parish church, their star,
cradled in a cluster of bent yews.

What's altered in the scene
isn't just the split sack of pesticide, blowing
from a hedge, the tractor waiting on the hill,
or the bare sting of my legs against the stalks;
it is my aimless pleasure in the walk
and the edge of melancholy it lends the bells
calling me to a hope I cannot enter
across fields I know well, yet do not know.

Iain Crichton Smith

Remembering

When the wind blows the curtains wide, do you not remember
the green trams on their wires and yourself young,
singing on a street that no one now can find.
It is as if the book opens, showing the parts you have played
in a theatre more precious to you than The Globe
with its ghostly flags flying in an Elizabethan wind.

Iain Crichton Smith

The Statue

The statue stands among the green leaves.
The face looks out through students' coloured scarves

across the shadows steadily towards Rome.
It remembers faintly the imperium

of bronze and horses. Now the freshening green
is all around it, and the students lean

nonchalantly against it. These beginnings
agitate the stone to precious longings,

an early dewy Rome more tentative than
that full-blown blossom, vicious and urbane.

1980

Anthony Hecht

Auspices

Cold, blustery cider weather, the flat fields
Bleached pale as straw, the leaves, such as remain,
Pumpkin or leather-brown. These are the wilds
Of loneliness, huge, vacant, sour and plain.

The sky is hourless dusk, portending rain.
Or perhaps snow. This narrow footpath edges
A small stand of scrub pine, warped as with pain,
And baneberry lofts its little poisoned pledges.

The footpath ends in a dried waterhole,
Plastered with black like old tar-paper siding.
The fearfullest desolations of the soul
Image themselves as local and abiding.

Even if I should get away from here
My trouser legs are stuck with burrs and seeds,
Grappled and spiked reminders of my fear,
Standing alone among the beggarweeds.

Anthony Thwaite

Waiting

All day the telephone in silence sits.
We are forgotten. The whole sky is blank.

I read a Kurdish poem: 'Nothing sadder
In early morning than to see stooped workmen
Building prisons'.
                    This is where we live,
Envied for what we have, for what they think we have.

Love isolates and binds, puts up its walls.
We are inviolate. The air is still.

From dawn till bedtime, nothing.
Jangle of keys beyond the outer gate.
Promises simmering, a lifetime's pause
High on the brink.
                    Whatever lies below
Covers its wings, folds over, falls asleep.
The telephone in curtained darkness sits.

1981

Tony Harrison

Currants

I

An Eccles cake's my *petite madeleine*!

On Sundays dad stoked up for next week's bake
and once took me along to be 'wi' t'men'.

One Eccles needs the currants you could take
in a hand imagined cupped round a girl's breast.
Between barrels of dried fruit and tubs of lard
I hunched and watched, and thought of girls undressed
and wondered what it meant when cocks got hard.
As my daydream dropped her silky underclothes,
from behind I smelt my father next to me.

Sweat dropped into the currants from his nose:

Go on! 'ave an 'andful. It's all free.

Not this barrel though. Your sweat's gone into it.
I'll go and get my handful from another.

I saw him poise above the currants and then spit:

Next Sunday you can stay 'ome wi' yer mother!

161

II

At dawn I hear him hawk up phlegm and cough
before me or my mother are awake.
He pokes the grate, makes tea, and then he's off
to stoke the ovens for my Eccles cake.

I smell my father, wallowing in bed,
dripping salt no one will taste into his dough,
and clouds of currants spiral in my head
and like drowsy autumn insects come and go
darkening the lightening skylight and the walls.

My veins grow out of me like tough old vines
and grapes, each bunch the weight of a man's balls
picked by toiling Greeks and Levantines,
are laid out somewhere open air and warm
where there might be also women, sun, blue sky

overcast as blackened currants swarm
into my father's hard 'flies' cemetery'.

(*Note:* An Eccles cake was called a 'flies' cemetery' by
children.)

Seamus Heaney

The Railway Children

When we climbed the slopes of the cutting
We were eye-level with the white cups
Of the telegraph poles and the sizzling wires.

Like lovely freehand they curved for miles
East and miles west beyond us, sagging
Under their burden of swallows.

We were small and thought we knew nothing
Worth knowing. We thought words travelled the wires
In the shiny pouches of raindrops,

Each one seeded full with the light
Of the sky, the gleam of the lines, and ourselves
So infinitesimally scaled

We could stream through the eye of a needle.

Philip Larkin

Bridge For The Living

(The words of a cantata composed by Anthony Hedges to celebrate
the opening of the Humber Bridge, first performed at the City Hall
in Hull on 11 April 1981)

Isolate city spread alongside water,
Posted with white towers, she keeps her face
Half-turned to Europe, lonely northern daughter,
Holding through centuries her separate place.

Behind her domes and cranes enormous skies
Of gold and shadows build; a filigree
Of wharves and wires, ricks and refineries,
Her working skyline wanders to the sea.

In her remote three-cornered hinterland
Long white-flowered lanes follow the riverside.
The hills bend slowly seaward, plain gulls stand,
Sharp fox and brilliant pheasant walk, and wide

Wind-muscled wheatfields wash round villages,
Their churches half-submerged in leaf. They lie
Drowned in high summer, cartways and cottages,
The soft huge haze of ash–blue sea close by.

Snow-thickened winter days are yet more still:
Farms fold in fields, their single lamps come on,
Tall church-towers parley, airily audible,
Howden and Beverley, Hedon and Patrington,

While scattered on steep seas, ice-crusted ships
Like errant birds carry her loneliness,
A lighted memory no miles eclipse,
A harbour for the heart against distress.

★

And now this stride into our solitude,
A swallow-fall and rise of one plain line,
A giant step for ever to include
All our dear landscape in a new design.

The winds play on it like a harp; the song,
Sharp from the east, sun-throated from the west,
Will never to one separate shire belong,
But north and south make union manifest.

Lost centuries of local lives that rose
And flowered to fall short where they began
Seem now to reassemble and unclose,
All resurrected in this single span,

Reaching for the world, as our lives do,
As all lives do, reaching that we may give
The best of what we are and hold as true:
Always it is by bridges that we live.

Peter Redgrove on

The Apple Broadcast[1]
(Routledge & Kegan Paul) 1981

A lot is said nowadays about the operation of the 'unconscious mind' in poetry. I would like to take a departure from the usual mode, and speak instead of the 'unconscious senses'. Aristotle assured us that we have only five senses: hearing, vision, smell, taste and touch. In fact we have many more: there are at least thirty different sense-qualities associated with touch alone; and it has been demonstrated recently that we can sense in some measure microwave emission (such as the moon gives off in plenty) and electrostatic and geomagnetic fields. We can also react with extraordinary subtlety to what are called 'pheromones', which are a cross between perfumes and super-active hormones, and are emitted by all kinds of being, including trees, dogs, and our fellow-humans. Now it is *ourselves*, what we usually call our 'conscious' minds, which are ordinarily unconscious of such influences, and which tend to relegate these gifts of sense to the supernatural ('vibes'), the animal (the 'mystery' of homing pigeons), the deprecated ('women's intuition'), or to poetic licence and the pathetic fallacy.

There are also unacknowledged inner senses and effectors. If you tape a thermometer to your thumb, and imagine strongly that you have dipped the hand in hot water, the temperature of the thumb will rise, visibly. You have told your thumb, via your imagination, to notice its natural warmth, and by attending to it, to alter it. This drawing upon capacities and sensory signals usually unnoticed, is called biofeedback, and with its aid you can learn to control heart rhythm, blood pressure, brain rhythms, etc., by means of imagined symbols and images. The act of imagination is a tuning device that alerts one's inner senses to real but previously unnoticed signals.[2]

I think that this may all pertain to a new view of the function of poetry. It is currently held that a poem must arise out of experience. True enough, but only half the story. A poem must also *give* you an experience. It may be one of a kind that you have never had before – but that is no reason for turning on the poet and saying he hasn't had it either! By the exercise of imagination through the entering into the images, symbols, diction, rhythms, fiction, thought of a poem, one notices and feels what one did not perceive before, both inwardly and out-wardly. The poem is a tuning or feedback device which alters or adjusts our capacity to respond to the world.

I am very pleased that my book *The Apple Broadcast* is the Choice; not only for the book's sake, but because this may indicate a swing of interest towards a type of poetry which I favour and try to write: the kind that makes us imagine unexpectedly, which helps us value beings and events we thought below notice, and which provides us with images and symbols that, re-imagined in this secu-lar world, can help some of the energy and attention flow that used to be thought exclusively religious.[3] Discussion of poetry along these lines has so far been infrequent in this country. It was an English author who proposed the idea of the Two Cultures, and it is in England that Science and Art have been kept rigidly apart. Yet it is easy to see, particularly nowadays, how Science and Imagina-tion must work together to give a modern account of the human universe. I myself believe that 'poetry, not aban-doning itself to the unconscious, but seizing it and raising it as far as possible into consciousness, . . . prefigures a final reconciliation of the two.'[4]

Notes:
[1] These ideas are now fully developed in *The Black Goddess and the Sixth Sense*, Bloomsbury. 1987.
[2] Robert M. Stern and William J. Ray: *Biofeedback: Potential and Limits*. University of Nebraska Press. 1980.
[3] Some aspects of these questions as raised in my own poetry are discussed in a series of articles in *Poetry Review* (Vol. 71, No. 2–3, Sept 81.)
[4] Angelo Philip Bertocci: *From Symbolism to Baudelaire*. Southern Illinois University Press. 1964. p. 39.

Penelope Shuttle

The Tree in the Yard

The red tree in the yard
fans out branches against the cob wall's whitewash.

The tree is Japanese and scarlet.
It is immune to the moods of the air.

At the window this early in the morning
light is not loud enough to be heard.

I look out at the tree
raw with berries.

I have no name for this tree.
It was here before we owned the yard,

and knew how to arrange its autumn redness
long ago:

and so I watch it,
almost unwieldy with its weight of berries
braced against the wall,
dealing with its own nature,

its red memory, scarlet conclusions.

This relapse into red,
the big blossoming before winter –
all so carefully designed, planned,
and then – idea abandoned to act.

For thoughts alone bring no fruit.

The tree exists in its red silence.
Loud birds rip at the fruit,
hungry black smoke of the berry bonfire.

Charles Tomlinson

From the Motorway

Gulls flock in to feed from the waste
   They are dumping, truck by truck,
Onto a hump of land three roads
   Have severed from all other:
Once the seeds drift down and net together
   This shifting compost where the gulls
Are scavenging a winter living,
   It will grow into a hill – for hawks
A hunting ground, but never to be named:
   No one will ever go there. How
Shall we have it back, a belonging shape?
   For it will breed no ghosts
But only – under the dip and survey
   Of hawk-wings – the bones of tiny prey,
Its sodium glow on winter evenings
   As inaccessible as Eden . . .

1982

Dannie Abse

Friends

Since our acorn days we've been friends
    but now at this oak door
I sense you do not wish me well.
    Why so, I cannot tell.

Though red carpet and silver gong
    may welcome us within,
friend, be yourself. Give me your hand.
    Come, this is what we planned.

Bitter as coloquintida
    a green lampshade in the hall
turns the light on your face to bile.
    Friend, turn to me and smile.

I too have felt envy and rage,
    cursed this stranger or that;
with needles in wax, cast a spell,
    damned him or her to hell,

yet never a friend, no, not one
    I would still call a friend.
Now you whom I thought to be loyal
    wish me under the soil.

Douglas Dunn

Empty Wardrobes

I sat in a dress shop, trying to look
As dapper as a young ambassador
Or someone who'd impressed me in a book,
A literary rake or movie star.

Clothes are a way of exercising love.
False? A little. And did she like it? Yes.
Days, days, romantic as Rachmaninov,
A ploy of style, and now not comfortless.

She walked out from the changing-room in brown,
A pretty smock with its embroidered fruit;
Dress after dress, a lady-like red gown
In which she flounced, a smart career-girl's suit.

The dress she chose was green. She found it in
Our clothes-filled cabin trunk. The pot-pourri,
In muslin bags, was full of where and when.
I turn that scent like a memorial key.

But there's that day in Paris, that I regret,
When I said No, franc-less and husbandly.
She browsed through hangers in the Lafayette,
And that comes back tonight, to trouble me.

Now there is grief the couturier, and grief
The needlewoman mourning with her hands,
And grief the scattered finery of life,
The clothes she gave as keepsakes to her friends.

James Fenton

Cambodia

One man shall smile one day and say goodbye.
Two shall be left, two shall be left to die.

One man shall give his best advice.
Three men shall pay the price.

One man shall live, live to regret.
Four men shall meet the debt.

One man shall wake from terror to his bed.
Five men shall be dead.

One man to five. A million men to one.
And still they die. And still the war goes on.

Andrew Motion

Writing

After what felt like a lifetime of rent
I bought somewhere my own. But at once,
in less than a week, he was writing:
Dear Madam, I hope you won't mind —

we met when I sold you the house.
It was mine. I gave you the china tea.
I showed you the room where you told me
yes, you could write in that room.

In the home I have now they are cruel.
There are traitors — and spies. I am hoping
my doctor is kind, but what is he doing
to bring me my wife, or give me her news?

Please, if this reaches you, tell her. Say —
if a visit is difficult, letters are fine.
Think of me reading this through at my desk,
throwing it down on my typewriter, frowning,

and wondering was this the room where she died?
Then think of my whisper to answer him:
Dearest heart. Forgive me. I'm ill
and dictating this. But I long for you always,

and when I'm recovered, I'll visit you.
Lazily spinning the phrases out, and finally
writing them, telling myself it was
kindness, and might even turn into love.

R. S. Thomas

Centuries

The fifteenth passes with drums and in armour;
the monk watches it through the mind's grating.

The sixteenth puts on its cap and bells
to poach vocabulary from a king's laughter.

The seventeenth wears a collar of lace
at its neck, the flesh running from thought's candle.

The eighteenth has a high fever and hot blood,
but clears its nostrils with the snuff of wit.

The nineteenth emerges from history's cave
rubbing its eyes at the glass prospect.

The twentieth is what it looked forward to
beating its wings at windows that are not there.

1983

Michael Hofmann

Bärli

Your salami breath tyrannized the bedroom
where you slept on the left, my mother, tidily,
on the right. I could cut the atmosphere with a knife:

the enthusiasm for spice, rawness, vigour,
in the choppy air. It was like your signature,
a rapid scrawl from the side of your pen –

individual, overwhelming, impossible –
a black Greek energy that cramped itself into
affectionate diminutives, *Dein Vati,* or *Papi.*

At forty, you had your tonsils out, child's play
with Little Bear nuns, Ursulines for nurses.
Hours after the operation, you called home . . .

humbled and impatient, you could only croak.
I shivered at your weakness – the faint breeze
that blew through you and formed words.

Peter Scupham

Genio Loci

Brick and mortar for the ghost
Slipped between our first and last,
That beneficence which came
When man called his hearth a home;
From a roaming wilderness
Cut the mystery of place.

Overhead the star-beasts pass
This loose gazebo, winter-house,
Patched with glass and cockle-shell,
Cobbled up with flint and tile,
Where the garden guardian
Hosts his feather, fur and fin,

And, as coloured lights go down,
Glazing rime upon the green,
As the winds blow colder through
Spaces leaded bough by bough,
Keeps at this dark terminus
The empty nest, the chrysalis.

Wendy Cope

Tich Miller

Tich Miller wore glasses
with elastoplast-pink frames
and had one foot three sizes larger than the other.

When they picked teams for outdoor games
she and I were always the last two
left standing by the wire-mesh fence.

We avoided one another's eyes,
stooping, perhaps, to re-tie a shoelace,
or affecting interest in the flight

of some fortunate bird, and pretended
not to hear the urgent conference:
'Have Tubby!' 'No, no, have Tich!'

Usually they chose me, the lesser dud,
and she lolloped, unselected,
to the back of the other team.

At eleven we went to different schools.
In time I learned to get my own back,
sneering at hockey-players who couldn't spell.

Tich died when she was twelve.

Ken Smith

Het Achterhuis

A glimpse: at the high window her face
a moment at a corner of the blind,
the frost forming its flower, in the garden
all the winter leaves so much leather,
so many tongues, scraps of old gossip.

For so little you can die: the price
on a second hand coat, a finger ring,
the brown shoes in the cupboard, the mirror
where your mother powders her face.
For these you will be taken.

Mice on the stairs, grey packets of dust.
The ice making its maps out of water.
On the square stones of the Prinsengracht
soldiers' boots tapping *links rechts links*.
In its season the chestnut's sudden blossom.

Alan Brownjohn

Box

It was really remarkable
You should ring after all these years . . .
I was on the brink of a quite
Momentous decision, I mean
A momentous *gaffe*, in my life;
And your call dragged me back from it
Like suddenly finding a room
Where I stood there at the window
And was just preparing to jump!

You cannot explain why you got
In touch? Well – *telepathy*, yes?
What else sent your hand racing out
To a telephone down in Strood
To release this bit of your past
Like a small, crated holy ghost
In Leeds? Your desire to explore
What things your past might be doing
By ringing it up was so *right*.

And there could be more out here, yes?
If you phoned me a second time?
Just dying for that little nudge
To enter the present and bring
New life – and old fascinations –
To a friend it recalled so well
(Who had clearly remembered *it*?)!
I am just like I was, you know,
Except this tiny bit older . . .

Aren't you awfully glad you rang?

Medbh McGuckian

Before the Wedding

I am the edge of a lawn trampled
By children if I searched and read
Forever I could not find again my
Place in sleep I've lost like a bookmark:
And just as there is something deliberate
Always in a roof's going from steel–grey
To green, so this is instead of flowers.

No puffy section of the moon meekly
Entering my fatal kitchen, or sunray
Rocking over what had once been a door,
Lets me stay beautifully aimless like
Unattended grass, probably forever
In every sense. I've seen a woman
To whom ten or even five years meant

A lot, now twirling death like a little
Spoon in her fingers or a heavy bag
From one hand to the other: no one but you
Tells her that perhaps she is departing
Too soon, tomorrow happens in the hour
After we fall asleep at night, when young
Kisses we have pushed beneath the ice

Of the sea, return to quicken the lake
Of the heart. Though I for one am hardly
Present in your dreams, that must be gardens
In themselves, some one will see them
With my rested eyes, with premarital
Precision in her passing voice, remark,
He is still entering, he is still in the doorway.

Carol Ann Duffy

The Race

They were never real eggs. The sun
was hotter then, round on a bright blue sky
like the way I painted it. My knees
wore different scabs all summer.

The winner stood on a beer crate, smirking,
whilst the others sulked. One year, I had a plan
and stole a fresh egg from our kitchen.
It was lighter, sat in the deep spoon safely.

Childhood is running forever for a faraway tape.
I was always last, but that day
sped away from the others, a running commentary
coming from nowhere in my head.

I was still in front when the egg fell,
leaving only sunlight in my spoon. I turned
as Junior 4 rushed past, ran back
and knelt to scoop the yolk up from the grass.

U. A. Fanthorpe

M.S.

There is a small dead tree in the aviary
For them to perch on. But the aviary's closed
(*Too cold yet, I suppose,* she says, though we're drinking
Tea in the garden.) Two and a half pair,

Dippers, rollers, a single red canary, waiting
To be found a mate; they have all chosen
To sing in their cage. From three in the morning
They're at it: opera, jazz, chorale –

Better, he says, *than yer nightingale, any day.*

I'd set 'em free, she tells me quietly, *only I know*
They wouldn't live. She sees I find her talk hard
To understand. Fine muscular control has left
Her lips and tongue. She pitches as she lumbers

The deck of her world, the trim new stairless house.
The canaries are nesting, their young are hatched.
She tells me she can't bear to look at them.
I watch her lifting her *stupid* left leg

Into a new position. He spends
A lot of time in the garden. The new small pond
Is his work, where the fine fat red fish swim.
Evening: the birds are chanting a sort of requiem.

Roy Fuller on

New and Collected Poems 1934–84

(Secker & Warburg) 1985

I sometimes say that the audience for new poetry has not increased in my adult lifetime. No doubt in this there is a strong element of an old man's desire to shock or leg-pull. But the thing is arguable.

The first poem in my *New and Collected Poems 1934–84* appeared in the December 1934 number of *New Verse*, the leading little poetry magazine of the day. I would estimate its then circulation at 1,200 copies. It was five years on before I managed to get my first book of poems published. Since R. A. Caton of the Fortune Press paid no royalties (or certainly not to me) the circulation of that lies buried in his archives – wherever they may be – but if three figures were reached it would be a marvel. The sales of the last book of mine represented in *New and Collected Poems* failed by a long chalk to reach four figures, and many of the pieces in the new poems section of the book appeared in periodicals with circulations much below that of the 1934 *New Verse*.

Has all the cash lavished on education and the arts during the last half century been without enduring effect in the sphere of poetry? It may be said that in educing my own example I have lit on a stubbornly unpopular poet, but I believe I am far from untypical – may well, indeed, be typical. Of course, the setting of certain poets as school texts, and bringing in contemporary literature for university study, has produced substantial sales for a few. However, except for the poets concerned, this seems to me to have had ludicrous results. The enormous repu-tation of Dylan Thomas and of a few other poets, still alive, coupled with examinees' sketchy knowledge of the rest of modern verse, is surely a very bad thing. The continuing minuscule circulation of poetry (and some general literary) magazines, even of outstanding excel-lence, is a measure of how far school and university education has been from the anticipated effect.

183

I was amused to read not long ago, in some article bemoaning poets' fate, words to the effect that of course Roy Fuller has no problems of dissemination; can simply choose some eminent publisher when sufficient material has been accumulated, and bob's your uncle. In fact, behind *New and Collected Poems* is a history of poetry publishing snakes and ladders, probably characteristic. The Fortune Press was a somewhat desperate *pis aller* after *Poems* (1939) had been turned down by goodness knows how many more conventional firms. John Lehmann, who published *Epitaphs and Occasions* (1949) went out of business in the harrowing manner related in his autobiographies; and *Counterparts* (1954) was rejected a good few times before Alan Ross introduced me to Derek Verschoyle. Alas, that firm (it as well unhesitatingly published two novels of mine, marvellous brief epoch) was also shot from under me, but luckily its assets and liabilities were taken over by André Deutsch, who published me until *The Reign of Sparrows* (1980), when once again Alan Ross, in the guise of London Magazine Editions, came to my rescue. Needless to say, the bulk of *New and Collected Poems* implies a heart-warming act of faith on the part of Secker and Warburg. I must add that the troublesome history thus related may be an encouragement to young (and old!) poets, rather than otherwise.

All this prompts the question: is your poetry wanted? Naturally, one who has been writing it for sixty years desires the answer to be in the affirmative, unless he is content to be an utter monomaniac. The larger question – is new poetry wanted? – must also get a yes, unless culture as previously known is to expire. But the audience for it looks like remaining tiny – the reverse of what we anticipated in the thirties: an audience growing with an ideal growth of further education; and with poetry itself becoming more demotic ('common speech', a characteristic syndrome). Ironically, as to demoticization, the ubiquity of *vers libre* may have militated against poetry's popularity by reducing its memorability.

Accordingly, it is crucial for the Poetry Book Society to continue to flourish. I have always believed it to be paramount among agencies designed to 'help' poetry (inverted commas, because the best help for poetry is for poets in general to write skilfully and sensibly, and for geniuses regularly to arise). During the many years I was on its Board I hoped its membership would reach and pass 1,000.[1] (This was not achieved until I had left the Board!) That magic figure just about makes publishing a new book of verse a plausible commercial proposition. If every member would also buy the PBS Recommendations that would mean other books, besides the Choice, falling into the viable category, and greatly encourage publishers (to say nothing of poets). That I urge members to do this as a regular habit is therefore not solely because the selectors have recommended me!

Note:[1] As we go to press membership stands at 1,800. ed.

Philip Larkin

Philip Larkin first President of the PBS, recalls Eric W. White, its first Secretary.

Eric White was Assistant Secretary of the Arts Council when I first knew him, which meant that his responsibilities were wider than simply literature, but when I joined what was then known as the Poetry Panel I soon saw what a hard worker he was in the cause of poetry, and subsequently for all forms of writing. He seemed to me possessed of great energy and enthusiasm, constantly travelling to meet new writers and new publishers, and I am sure that a reading of the minutes would confirm that he did a great deal to assist what was stirring and germinating in literature in the sixties and afterwards.

He was an excellent committee man, guiding the Chairman without seeming to, and I have remembered (and sometimes used) his habit of proposing in a wide-eyed way (as if it had just occurred to him) something that he had been planning for several weeks ('How would it be if–'). I shall always be grateful to him for taking up the important question of the retention in this country of British literary manuscripts, which he did so much to foster.

Eric was my first introduction to 'metropolitan literature', and I am afraid I always found him slightly comical, but was consoled by the belief that he was perfectly well aware of this, and it amused him to startle my provincial attitudes. In retrospect I think he was both tough and kind, a rare combination in a rare man.

E. J. Scovell

A Present of Sea Shells

The shells are elaborate and curious
Like human thought, and yet not thoughts of ours.
A young boy searched them out on an island's shores
Where shells so perfect are not plentiful,
And in a carton, wrapped in cotton wool,
Sent them through air across the world to us,

Knowing that, settled far inland, we still
Love the sea's gifts, complex and beautiful.
This fact, this node of facts, in thought (like a shell
In the hand) I hold – the boy on the shore, the sun
On the wings of the mind-powered great machine homing in.
Time yields its patterned shells, none, none identical.

Waking in dark on the flat-lands of the night
To sadness, or space too vast, I light this light:
The boy designing our pleasure; and now, spread out
On a tray, the shells from their journeying. One is a dawn
                                                    that pales,
One etched with finest fans on lapping scales,
One whorled; orange and green seem hand-strewn over it.

George Szirtes

from *The Photographer in Winter*

What awful cold we seem to have had this year.
A winter of betrayals. Even words
Drop dead in flight, and, afterwards,
We try to sweep them up, quite uselessly.
I can hardly see a hand in front of me.
Everything is speckled. Nothing is clear.

Imagine trying to focus through this swirl
And cascade of snow. It's dark already.
Impossible to keep the picture steady
In the wind. An early evening filters in
Behind the white – my gloves are much too thin
To keep it out. I think I am a girl.

'To be alone in winter is like dying,'
She sings. Here everyone is alone. We die
Of the cold. It can be dangerous to cry
When tears freeze on your cheeks. We must have courage
And think of winter as a happy marriage,
The kiss of snow, the wind's contented sighing.

We must have courage till the spring regains
Her confidence. Courage is everything.
I load the camera and slowly bring
The landscape into focus. My heart stutters
But my hand is firm, and as I click the shutter
I feel the cold blood thawing in my veins.

1986

George Barker

In Memoriam E.S.

Ah most unreliable of all women of grace
in the breathless hurry of your leave-taking
you forgot – you forgot for ever – our last embrace.

Graham Greene

World War Three

It was at best a small affair,
I had never heard of the island,
I had no intention of dying there
For a people I didn't know.

The radio talked of a greater affair,
Moscow gone and London destroyed,
I had to patrol the island there
For a people I didn't know.

The war I knew was a small affair,
I had never heard of the island,
I died of a snake bite in the bush
For a people I didn't know.

Graham Greene

Go-Slow

It was go-go-slow at Clapham Junction,
it was go-slow by the clock,
yet how swift the hours that I waited there
would have seemed to the man from the dock.

I was one of a crowd on the centre platform,
while three hours passed on the clock,
but no one bothered to notice me there
as they'd noticed the man from the dock.

The longest go-slow at Clapham Junction
was half an hour by the clock,
when they laughed at Wilde as he waited there
in handcuffs fresh from the dock.

Derek Mahon

Achill

im chaonaí uaigneach nach mór go bhfeicim an lá

I lie and imagine a first light gleam in the bay
    After one more night of erosion and nearer the grave,
Then stand and gaze from a window at break of day
    As a shearwater skims the ridge of an incoming wave;
And I think of my son a dolphin in the Aegean,
    A sprite among sails knife-bright in a seasonal wind,
And wish he were here where currachs walk on the ocean
    To ease with his talk the solitude locked in my mind.

I sit on a stone after lunch and consider the glow
    Of the sun through mist, a pearl bulb containèdly fierce;
A rain-shower darkens the schist for a minute or so
    Then it drifts away and the sloe-black patches disperse.
Croagh Patrick towers like Naxos over the water
    And I think of my daughter at work on her difficult art
And wish she were with me now between thrush and plover,
    Wild thyme and sea-thrift, to lift the weight from my heart.

The young sit smoking and laughing on the bridge at evening
    Like birds on a telephone pole or notes on a score.
A tin whistle squeals in the parlour, once more it is raining,
    Turfsmoke inclines and a wind whines under the door;
And I lie and imagine the lights going on in the harbour
    Of white-housed Náousa, your clear definition at night,
And wish you were here to upstage my disconsolate labour
    As I glance through a few thin pages and switch off the light.

Craig Raine

Heaven on Earth

Now that it is night,
you fetch in the wash
from outer space,

from the frozen garden
filmed like a kidney,
with a ghost in your mouth,

and everything you hold,
two floating shirts,
towels, tablecloth, a sheet,

ignores the law of gravity.

Only this morning,
the wren at her millinery,
making a baby's soft bonnet,

as we stopped by the spring,
watching the water
well up in the grass,

as if the world
was teething.
It was heaven on earth

and it was only the morning.

Acknowledgments

The editors of the annual PBS anthologies from which much of this anthology has been selected were: G. S. Fraser 1956; Vernon Watkins 1957; Patric Dickinson 1958; James Reeves 1959; Donald Davie 1960; John Fuller 1962; Alan Ross 1963; Roy Fuller 1964; Francis Hope 1965; Eric W. White 1966; Martin Dodsworth 1969; John Fuller 1970; Terry Eagleton 1971; Dannie Abse 1972; Charles Osborne 1973; Philip Larkin 1974; Dannie Abse 1975; Colin Falck 1977; Patricia Beer 1978; Douglas Dunn 1979; Peter Porter 1980; Andrew Motion 1981; Alan Brownjohn 1982; David Harsent 1983; Gavin Ewart 1984; Carol Rumens 1985; Jonathan Barker 1986.

The PBS publication in which each poem or prose item appeared follows immediately in brackets after the copyright note. Abbreviations used are: B Bulletin, S annual Supplementary anthology, F Festival programme.

For permission to reprint copyright material the publishers gratefully acknowledge the following:

Hutchinson, an imprint of Century Hutchinson Ltd for 'Friends' from *Ask the Bloody Horse* by Dannie Abse (S); Oxford University Press for 'Think Before You Shoot' from *Selected Poems* by Fleur Adcock, 1983 (S); Hutchinson, an imprint of Century Hutchinson Ltd for 'Creeper' from *Collected Poems 1944–1979* by Kingsley Amis (B); Faber & Faber Ltd for 'The More Loving One' and 'River Profile' from *Collected Poems* by W. H. Auden (S) (S); Faber & Faber Ltd for 'The clock is banging' from 'The Golden Chains' from *Collected Poems* by George Barker (S); the author for 'In Memoriam E.S.' and the prose on *The View from a Blind I* by George Barker (S) (B); Peterloo Poets for 'Surgery' from *A Lifetime of Dying* by Elizabeth Bartlett, 1979 (S) and 'Great House on View Day' from *A House Under Old Sarum* by Joan Barton, 1981 (S); Hutchinson, an imprint of Century Hutchinson Ltd for 'Prochorus Thompson' from *Selected Poems* by Patricia Beer (S); Peter Porter for 'Running Mad' by Martin Bell (S); John G. Murray and the Trustees of Sir John Betjeman's Estate for the prose on *Summoned by Bells* by John Betjeman (B); Hutchinson, an imprint of Century Hutchinson Ltd for 'A Broken Image' from *Selected Poems* by Thomas Blackburn (B); the author and Chatto & Windus for 'Culloden' from *The Year of the Whale* by George Mackay Brown (S); Hutchinson, an imprint of Century Hutchinson for 'Box' from *The Old Flea-Pit* by Alan

Brownjohn (S); the author for 'Welsh Love Letter' by Michael Burn (S); Jane Aiken Hodge for 'The Compassionate Fool' by Norman Cameron (B); the author and Macmillan for 'The Whangbird' and 'Infant Song' from *Collected Poems* by Charles Causley (S) (S); the author for 'Carmel' by Jack Clemo (S); Bloodaxe Books Ltd for 'Visiting Hour' by Stewart Conn (S); Faber & Faber Ltd for 'Tich Miller' from *Making Cocoa for Kingsley Amis* by Wendy Cope (S); the author for 'To Helen Keller' by Donald Davie (S); the Executors of the Estate of C. Day Lewis and Jonathan Cape Ltd for 'Lot 96' from *Pegasus and Other Poems* by C. Day Lewis (S); the Literary Trustees of Walter de la Mare and the Society of Authors as their representative for 'Ulysses' and 'Shepherd's Warning' by Walter de la Mare (S) (S); the author for 'The Race' by Carol Ann Duffy (S); Faber & Faber Ltd for 'Empty Wardrobes' from *Elegies* by Douglas Dunn (S); the author for the prose on *Terry Street* by Douglas Dunn (B); Faber & Faber Ltd for 'Incognito' from *Collected Poems* by Lawrence Durrell (B); Mrs Valerie Eliot and Faber & Faber Ltd for T. S. Eliot's remarks at a Press Conference of the Poetry Book Society, April 10th 1956 and subsequently incorporated in 'Poetry and the Schools', and Introduction to Festival of Poetry Programme from uncollected writings by T. S. Eliot (B) (F); the author for 'Seaside Sensation' from *Collected Poems 1987*, Oxford University Press by D. J. Enright (S); Hutchinson, an imprint of Century Hutchinson Ltd for 'Huckstep' from *The Collected Ewart, 1933–1980* by Gavin Ewart (S); Peterloo Poets for 'M. S.' from *A Watching Brief* by U. A. Fanthorpe, 1987 (S); A. D. Peters & Co Ltd for 'Cambodia' by James Fenton (B); Oxford University Press for 'On the Open Side' from *Poems 1955–1980* by Roy Fisher, 1980 (S); Martin Secker & Warburg Ltd for 'Buffalo' from 'Landscapes of Western New York' from *Selected Poems 1954–1982* by John Fuller (S); Martin Secker & Warburg Ltd for 'Twenty Years of the Poetry Book Society' & 'The Same After Twenty-Five Years' from *New and Collected Poems 1934–84* by Roy Fuller (B); the author for the prose on *New and Collected Poems 1934–84* by Roy Fuller (B); Nessie Graham for 'The Coastguard's Poem' by W. S. Graham (S); A. P. Watt Ltd on behalf of the Executors of the Estate of Robert Graves for 'The Meeting' and the prose on *New Poems 1962* by Robert Graves (B) (B); the author for 'World War Three' and 'Go-Slow' by Graham Greene (S) (S); the Estate of Geoffrey Grigson for 'Academic Futures' from *Discoveries of Bones and Stones* Macmillan by Geoffrey Grigson (S); Faber & Faber Ltd for 'A Waking Dream' from *The Passages of Joy* by Thom Gunn (S); the author for the prose on *Moly* by Thom Gunn (B); the author for 'The Glade' from *Collected Poems 1941–83* Carcanet, 1984 by Michael Hamburger (S); Faber & Faber Ltd for 'Windfalls' from *The Visit* by Ian Hamilton (S); the author for 'Currants' from *Selected*

Faber & Faber Ltd for 'The One Desire' from *Why Brownlee Left* by Paul Muldoon (S); the Estate of Norman Nicholson for 'Have You Been to London?' from *A Local Habitation*, Faber & Faber Ltd by Norman Nicholson (S); Unwin Hyman Ltd for 'Little Johnny's Final Letter' from *Little Johnny's Confession* by Brian Patten (S); Faber & Faber Ltd for 'Hidden Face' from *The Strange Museum* by Tom Paulin (S); the author for 'In the Open' by Ruth Pitter (B); Olwyn Hughes for 'Tulips' from *Collected Poems* by Sylvia Plath published by Faber & Faber Ltd (F); Jonathan Cape Ltd on behalf of the Estate of William Plomer for 'A Summer Storm' from *Collected Poems* by William Plomer (F); Oxford University Press for 'A Minor Lear' from *Collected Poems* by Peter Porter, 1983 (F); the author for the prose on *The Cost of Seriousness* by Peter Porter (B); the author for 'Heaven on Earth' and the prose on *A Martian Sends a Postcard Home* by Craig Raine (S) (B); Allen & Unwin for 'For the Bride' from *Collected Poems* by Kathleen Raine (B); the author for 'Philosophical Padding', 'Just Because My Teeth Are Pearly' and 'Not a Step Do I Stir Until That Cat's Back To Its Colour' by Tom Raworth (S) (S) (S); Martin Secker & Warburg Ltd for 'Early Morning Call' from *Fiction* by Peter Reading (S); the author for 'The Curiosity-Shop' and the prose on *The Apple Broadcast* by Peter Redgrove (S) (B); Heinemann & the Executors of the Estate of James Reeves for 'A Sonata by Handel' by James Reeves (B); Canongate Publishing Ltd for 'Outlook, Uncertain' from *Weathering* by Alastair Reid (S); the author and Chatto & Windus for 'Almost in Walking Distance' from *Unplayed Music* by Carol Rumens (S); Robson Books Ltd for 'The Loving Game' from *The Loving Game* by Vernon Scannell (S); Carcanet Press Ltd for 'A Present of Sea Shells' from *Collected Poems* by E. J. Scovell (S); Oxford University Press for 'Genio Loci' from *Out Late* by Peter Scupham, 1986 (S); Oxford University Press for 'The Tree in the Yard' from *The Child Stealer* by Penelope Shuttle, 1983 (S); Carcanet Press Ltd for 'The Skull and Cross-bones' from *Collected Poems 1943–1983*, 1984 by C. H. Sisson (S); the author for 'Remembering' and 'The Statue' by Iain Crichton Smith (S) (S); Bloodaxe Books Ltd for 'Het Achterhuis' from *Terra*, 1986 by Ken Smith (S); James MacGibbon for 'Heartless', 'Tenuous and Precarious', 'v.', 'Yes, I know' from *Collected Poems of Stevie Smith*, Penguin Modern Classics by Stevie Smith (S) (F) (S) (S); Oxford University Press for 'The Rendezvous' from *Collected Poems* by Bernard Spencer edited by Roger Bowen, 1981 (B); Faber & Faber Ltd for 'A Girl Who Has Drowned Herself Speaks' from *Collected Poems 1928–1985* by Stephen Spender (S); the author for 'Inscriptions' by Stephen Spender (Holograph poem); Oxford University Press for 'Blind Man and Child' from *Minute by Glass Minute* by Anne Stevenson, 1982 (S); Martin Secker & Warburg Ltd for the extract from

Index

Index of poems and prose by author and poems by title

202

203